The Greater Key of Solomon

ISBN: 978-1-63923-186-7

Printed: March 2022

Cover Art By: Amit Paul

Published and Distributed By: Lushena Books
607 Country Club Drive, Unit E
Bensenville, IL 60106
www.lushenabooksinc.com/books

ISBN: 978-1-63923-186-7

Notice To The Reader

In order to make it easy for the student to understand how to make the Pentacles shown over the figures in this book, it was necessary to change the position of certain pages. By turning to page 57 it will be noticed that pages 59 and 60 have been put between pages 57 and 58 instead of between 58 and 61. This was done, as explained above, in order to bring those pages which contain certain figures near the printed pages which explain the figures. In going through the book it may appear at the first glance that certain pages have been left out, but, upon investigation, it will be found that this is not true, for while there are no numbers shown in the book for pages 59, 60, 65, 66, 69, 70, 73, 74, 77, 78, 99 and 100, nothing has been left out of the reading matter, for the reason that these were illustrated pages showing the figures with the Pentacles above them, and instead of their being placed according to their number they were carried forward or set back in order to get them near the reading matter which gave directions for making the Pentacles shown on them. The above arrangement holds good throughout the book in general.

Instead of there being any pages left out of this book, it will be noticed that there have been many pages added, several extra ones having been inserted by the use of half numbers, and that 61½ and 62½ are between 63 and 64, while 63½ is between 67 and 68, 66½ and 67½ are between 71 and 72, 68½ and 69½ are between 75 and 76, 86½ and 87½ are between 97 and 98. These extra pages were added in order to make everything plain to the student, and to avoid confusion. In studying this book it will be found that the reading matter is complete; and that not one word has been left out of it, ALL the printed pages have been placed exactly where they belong, while the illustrated pages, containing the Pentacles, Seals and Talismans, have been placed so as to make them most convenient for the student.

It should be borne in mind that this famous book is a translation of ancient manuscripts and that the manner in which the book has been translated and put together is a piece of literary work seldom found in the English language; its author having been very painstaking and careful to convey to the student the true sense of the original manuscript, and this translation shows that it has not been thrown together without order, as is often the case with other translators, but that a complete order runs through the Volume from beginning to end.

THE PUBLISHERS.

The Greater Key Of Solomon

PREFACE TO BOOK ONE.

In presenting this celebrated Magical work to the *Disciple* of *Occultism* some few prefatory remarks are necessary.

The Key of Solomon, save for a curtailed and incomplete copy published in France in the seventeenth century, has never yet been printed, but has for centuries remained in *Manuscript* form inaccessible to all but the few fortunate scholars to whom the inmost recesses of the great libraries were open. I therefore consider that I am highly honored in being the individual to whose lot it has fallen to edit and publish the American Edition.

The fountain-head and storehouse of *Qabalistical Magic,* and the origin of much of the *Ceremonial Magic* of *Mediæval* times, the "Key" has been ever valued by *Occult* writers as a work of the highest authority; and notably in our own day *Eliphaz Lévi* has taken it for the model on which his celebrated *"Dogme et Rituel de la Haute Makie"* was based. It must be evident to the initiated reader of Lévi, that The Key of Solomon was his text book of study, and at the end of this volume I give a fragment of an ancient Hebrew *Manuscript* of The Key of Solomon, translated and published in the *"Philosophie Occulte,"* as well as an Invocation called the *"Qabalistical Invocation of Solomon,"* which bears close analogy to one in the First Book, being constructed in the same manner on the scheme of the *Sephiroth.*

The history of the Hebrew original of The Key of Solomon is given in the Introductions, but there is every reason to suppose that this has been entirely lost, and Christian, the pupil of *Lévi,* says as much in his "*Histoire de la Magie.*"

I see no reason to doubt the tradition which assigns the authorship of the "Key" to King Solomon, for among others *Josephus,* the Jewish historian, especially mentions the magical works attributed to that monarch; this is confirmed by many Eastern traditions, and his magical skill is frequently mentioned by the *Old Adepts.*

There are, however, two works on *Black Magic,* the "*Grimorium Verum,*" and the "*Clavicola di Salomone ridolta,*" which have been attributed to SOLOMON, and which have been in some cases especially mixed up with the present work; but which have nothing really to do therewith; they are full of evil magic, and I cannot caution the practical student too strongly against them.

There is also another work called "*Lemegeton, or the Lesser Key of Solomon the King,*" which is full of seals of various Spirits, and is not the same as the present book, though extremely valuable in its own department.

In editing this *Volume* I have omitted one or two experiments partaking largely of *Black Magic,* and which had evidently been derived from the two *Goetic* works mentioned above; I must further caution the practical worker against the use of blood; the prayer, the *Pentacle,* and the perfumes, or TEMPLE INCENSE, rightly used, are sufficient as the former verges dangerously on the evil path. Let him who, in spite of the warnings of this *Volume,* determines to work evil, be assured that evil will recoil on himself and that he will be struck by the reflex current.

This work is edited from several ancient MSS. in the *British Museum,* which all differ from each other in various points, some giving what is omitted by the others, but all unfortunately agreeing in one thing, which is the execrable mangling of the Hebrew words through the ignorance of the transcribers. But it is in the *Pentacles* that the Hebrew is worse, the letters being so vilely scribbled as to be actually undecipherable in some instances, and it has been part of my work for several years to correct and reinstate the proper Hebrew and Magical characters in the *Pentacles.* The student may therefore safely rely on their being now as nearly correct in their present reproduction as it is possible for them to be. I have, therefore, wherever I could, corrected the Hebrew of the Magical Names in the *Conjurations* and *Pentacles;* and in the few instances where it was not possible to do so, I have put them in the most usual form; carefully collating throughout one MS. with another. The Chapters are a little differently classed in the various MSS., in some instances the matter contained in them being transposed, &c. I have added notes wherever necessary.

The MSS. from which this work is edited are:—Add. MSS., 10,862: Sloane MSS., 1307 and 3091; Harleian MSS., 3981; King's MSS., 288: and Lansdowne MSS., 1202 and 1203; seven *codices* in all.

Of all these 10,862 Add. MSS. is the oldest, its date being about the end of the sixteenth century; 3981 Harleian is probably about the middle of the seventeenth century; the others of rather later date.

Add. MSS. 10,862 is written in contracted Latin, and is hard to read, but it contains Chapters which are omitted in the others and also an important Introduction. It is more concise in its wording. Its title is short, being simply THE KEY OF SOLOMON, translated from the Hebrew language into the Latin. An exact copy of the signature of the writer of this MS. is given in *Figure* 93.

3981 Harleian MSS.; 288 King's MSS.; and 3091 Sloane MSS., are similar, and contain the same matter and nearly the same wording; but the latter MS. has many errors of transcription. They are all in French. The *Conjurations* and wording of these are much fuller than in 10,862 Add. MSS. and 1202 Lansdowne MSS. The title is THE KEY OF SOLOMON, *King of the Hebrews,* translated from the Hebrew Language into Italian by *Abraham Colorno,* by the order of his most Serene Highness of Mantua; and recently put into French. The *Pentacles* are much better drawn, are in colored inks, and in the case of 3091 Sloane MSS., gold and silver are employed.

1307 Sloane MSS. is in Italian; its Title is "*La Clavicola di Salomone Redotta et epilogata nella nostra materna lingua del dottissimo Gio Peccatrix.*" It is full of Black Magic, and is a jumble of THE KEY OF SOLOMON proper, and the two Black Magic books before mentioned. The *Pentacles* are badly drawn. It, however, gives part of the Introduction to 10,862 Add. MSS., and is the only other MS. which does, save the beginning of another Italian version which is bound up with the former MS., and bears the title "*Zecorbenei.*"

1202 Lansdowne MSS. is "THE TRUE KEYS OF KING SOLOMON," by Armadel. It is beautifully written, with painted initial letters, and the *Pentacles* are carefully drawn in colored inks. It is more concise in style, but omits several Chapters. At the end are some short extracts from the *Grimorium Verum* with the *Seals* of evil spirits, which, as they do not belong to THE KEY OF SOLOMON proper, I have not given. For the evident classification of the "KEY" is in two books and no more.

1203 Lansdowne MSS. is "*The Veritable Keys of Solomon*" translated from the Hebrew into the Latin language by the Rabbin Agognazar. It is in French, exquisitely written in printing letters, and the *Pentacles* are carefully drawn in colored inks. Though containing similar matter to the others, the arrangement is utterly different; being all in one book, and not even divided into chapters.

The antiquity of the *Planetary Sigils* is shown by the fact that, among the *Gnostic Talismans* in the *British Museum,* there is a ring of copper with the *Sigils* of *Venus,* which are exactly the same as those given by the *Mediæval* writers on Magic.

Where *Psalms* are referred to I have in all instances given the English and not the Hebrew numbering of them.

In some places I have substituted the word AZOTH for "*Alpha and Omega,*" *e. g.*, on the blade of the *Knife* with the *Black Hilt, Figure* 62. I may remark that the *Magical Sword* may, in many cases, be used instead of the Knife.

In conclusion I will only mention, for the benefit of non-*Hebraists,* that Hebrew is written from right to left, and that from the consonantal nature of the *Hebrew Alphabet,* it will require fewer letters than in English to express the same word.

L. W. de LAURENCE.

Chicago, Ill., U. S. A., 1916.

SOLOMON, THE "WISE MAN"

BY L. W. de LAURENCE

Solomon, Son of David and Bathsheba (1033-975 B.C.); King of Israel; noted for his Wisdom and deep Knowledge of *Occult Forces;* author of the "Key of Solomon".

Solomon was a King, the son of a King; the wise son of a wise father; a righteous man's righteous child.

David, the father of Solomon, reigned for forty years, as it is written, "*And the days that David governed Israel were forty years.*"

Of Solomon, it is written, "And Solomon reigned in Jerusalem over all Israel forty years."

Solomon was born in the year 2912 A.M., and reigned over *Israel* forty years. Four hundred and thirty-three years elapsed between the date of Solomon's reign and that of the *Temple's* destruction.

"*Seest thou a man that is diligent in his work? Before kings may he place himself; let him not place himself before obscure men.*" (Prov. 22:29.)

In this verse Solomon alludes to himself. He built *King Solomon's Temple* in seven years, while he occupied fourteen years in erecting his *Palace.* Not because his *Palace* was more elegant or more elaborate in its workmanship than was the *Temple,* but because he was diligent in his work to finish the *Holy Temple,* while his own house could await time and opportunity.

Four cases of comparative righteousness between fathers and children may be noted:

First. A righteous man begets a righteous son.

Second. A wicked man begets a wicked son.

Third. A wicked man begets a righteous son.

Fourth. A righteous man begets a wicked son.

To each of these cases we may find a Biblical allusion; to each of them we may apply a parable and a proverb.

In reference to the righteous father and the righteous son, we find the following verse (*Psalm* 45:17): "*Instead of thy fathers shall be thy children.*" And we may apply the parable of the good fig tree which brought forth luscious fruit.

In reference to the wicked father and the wicked son we have in *Numbers* 32:14: "*And now behold, ye are risen up in your father's stead, a new race of sinful men.*"

Ancient is the proverb, "*From the wicked proceedeth wickedness*"; and applicable, the parable of the serpent bringing forth an asp.

In the third case, the wicked father begets a righteous son, as it is written, *"Instead of the thorn shall come up the fir tree."* And to this can we apply the *parable* of the rose budding on the bramble bush.

Lastly, a righteous man has a wicked son, as it is written, *"Instead of wheat, thorns came forth."* (*Job* 21:40.) And we have also the *parable* of the atttractive peach tree which brought forth bitter fruit.

SOLOMON was a king, the son of a King; the wise son of a wise father; a righteous man's righteous child. All the incident's in DAVID'S life, all his characteristics were paralleled in the life of SOLOMON.

DAVID reigned for forty years, as it is written, *"And the days that David governed Israel were forty years."*

Of SOLOMON it is written, *"And* SOLOMON *reigned in Jerusalem over all Israel forty years."* DAVID expressed himself by "words," as it is written, *"And these are the last words of David."*

SOLOMON likewise expressed himself by "words."

"The words of Koheleth the son of David." (*Eccles.* 1:1.)

DAVID said, "All is *vanity"*; as it is written, "For *vanity* only do all men make a noise." (*Psalm* 39:7.)

SOLOMON expressed himself with the same word, *"vanity." "Vanity* of *vanities,* saith Koheleth." (*Eccles.* 1:2.)

David wrote books, viz.: the five books of *Psalms;* and SOLOMON wrote four books: *Proverbs, Ecclesiastes,* the *Song of Solomon,* and *The Key of Solomon.*

David composed songs: *"And David spoke unto the Lord the words of this song."* (*Samuel* 22:1.)

SOLOMON also composed a song: *"The song of songs,"* which is SOLOMON'S.

He was the wise king alluded to in *Proverbs* 16:23, *"The heart of the wise maketh his mouth intelligent, and upon his lips increaseth information."* Meaning that the heart of the wise is full of knowledge and understanding; but this is shown to the world through the words of his mouth. And, by uttering with his lips the thoughts of his mind (or heart) he increases the information of the people. If a man possessing brilliant diamonds and precious stones, keeps his jewels concealed, no one is aware of their value; but if he allows them to be seen, their worth becomes known, and the pleasure of ownership is enhanced.

Applying this comparison to the case of SOLOMON, while his wisdom was locked up in his own breast it was of value to no one; but when he had given to the world his four books, men became acquainted with his great abilities. The words of his lips increased the information of his people, and so great was his reputation that any one in doubt concerning the meaning of a Biblical passage sought the king for an interpretation.

Not only in sacred lore did he raise the standard of education. He had mastered and taught the sciences of *Natural Philosophy, Physiology, Botany, Agriculture, Mathematics* in all its branches, *Occultism, Astronomy, Chemistry,* and in fact all useful studies. He also taught *Rhetoric* and the rules of *Poesy*. In *Occultism and "Talismanic Magic"* he was an *Adept.*

And in addition to this that Koheleth was wise, he continually taught the people knowledge.

If what others said interested the people, how much more readily did they listen to SOLOMON; with how much more ease did they comprehend him!

We may illustrate his method of teaching by the following comparison: There was a basket without ears, filled with fine fruit, but the owner was unable to get it to his home on account of the difficulty in carrying it, until a wise man, seeing the predicament, attached handles to the basket, when it could be carried with great ease.

So did SOLOMON remove difficulties from the path of the student.

Rabbi Huna further illustrated this same thing. "There was once," he said, "a well of most pure and excellent water; but the well was so deep that the people were not able to reach the water, until a man of wisdom, taking a bucket, attached to it one rope after another until the whole was long enough to reach the water. So was it with SOLOMON's teachings. The Bible is a well of truth, but its teachings are too deep for the understanding of some. SOLOMON, however, introduced parables and proverbs suited to the comprehension of all, through which means a knowledge of the law became readily obtainable."

Rabbi Simon, the son of Chalafta, related the following parable: "A certain king had an officer to whom he was much attached, and whom he took great delight in honoring. One day he said to this favorite, Come, express a wish; anything that I can give thee shall be thine.' Then this officer thought, 'If I ask the king for gold or silver or precious stones, he will give what I ask; even though I desire higher honor and more exalted station he will grant it, yet I will ask him for his daughter, for if he grants that, all the rest will be included.'"

When the Lord appeared to SOLOMON in *Gibon,* and said to him in a dream, *"What shall I give to thee?"* SOLOMON reflected, *"If I ask for gold, silver, or jewels, the Lord will give them to me; I will ask, however, for wisdom; if that is granted me, all other good things are included."* Therefore, he replied, *"Give to thy servant an understanding heart."*

Then said the Lord:

"Because thou hast asked for wisdom, and requested not wealth or dominion over thy enemies; by thy life, wisdom and knowledge shall be thine, and through them thou shalt obtain wealth and power."

"And Solomon awoke, and behold it was a dream." He wandered into the fields, and he heard the voices of the animals; the ass brayed, the lion roared, the dog barked, the rooster crowed, and behold he understood what they said, one to the other.

An ox, even after being killed and dressed, may be made to stand, provided the sinews are uncut; but if they are severed, cords are required to hold the body together. While SOLOMON remained free from sin his prayers were granted him for his own sake, but when he departed from the righteous way, the Lord said to him, *"For the sake of David, my servant, I will not take the kingdom from thee in thy lifetime."*

SOLOMON said, *"Vanity of vanities; vanity, even as a shadow."* A shadow of what nature? The shadow of a tower or a tree remains the shadow for a while, and then is lost, but the shadow of a bird flieth away, and there is neither bird nor shadow. DAVID said, *"Our days are as a passing shadow,"* and Rabbi Huna said, *"Our days pass quickly from us, even as the shadow of a flying bird."*

With the word vanity, SOLOMON expresses seven stages of a man's life.

The infant he compares to a king; riding in his little coach, and being kissed, admired, and praised by all. The child of three or four years he compares to a pig, fond of the dirt and soiling itself with its food. The child of ten is fond of dress; the youth adorns himself and seeks a wife; the married man is bold as the dog in seeking a livelihood for himself and family; and the old man he likens to an ape.

"God gave Wisdom to Solomon."

When SOLOMON was about building the temple, he applied to the King of *Egypt* for men to aid him in the work. *Pharaoh,* consulting his *Astrologers,* selected those men who were to die within the year. When they arrived at *Jerusalem* the wise SOLOMON sent them back at once. With each man he sent a shroud, and directed them to say to their master, "If *Egypt* is too poor to supply shrouds for her dead, and for that purpose sends them to me, behold here they are, the men and the shrouds together; take them and bury thy dead."

He was wiser than all other men, wiser even than Adam, who gave names to all the animals of the world, and even to himself, saying, "From the dust of the ground I was formed, and therefore shall my name be *Adam." Rabbi Tanchum* said, "Where is thy wisdom and thy understanding, O King SOLOMON? Thy words not only contradict themselves, but also the words of DAVID, thy father. He said, *'Not the dead can praise the Lord'* (*Psalm* 115:17), and thou didst say, *'Thereupon praised I the dead that are already dead, more than the living who are still alive.'* (*Eccles.* 4:2.) And thou didst also say, *'For a living dog fareth better than a dead lion.'"* (*Ibid.* 9:4.)

These seeming contradictions, however, may be readily explained. DAVID said, "Not the dead can praise the Lord," meaning that we should study God's law during life, as after its cessation 'twould be impossible. SOLOMON said, "Thereupon praised I the dead that are already dead." When the children of *Israel* sinned in the wilderness, MOSES prayed for them for their own sakes, and his prayer was unanswered; but when he said, *"Remember Abraham, and Isaac, and Israel, Thy servants,"* he met with a prompt reply. Therefore did not SOLOMON speak well in saying,

"Praise the dead that are already dead"? Take another instance: A king may decree laws, but many of his subjects may disregard them. Sometimes these laws, even if earnestly observed during the life of the one who made them, may be repealed or become obsolete after his death. MOSES, however, made many stringent laws, which have been observed through all generations. Therefore, SOLOMON said well, *"Thereupon will I praise the dead."*

Rabbi Judah, in the name of *Rab,* further explained this verse. He said, "What is the meaning of the following passage? 'Show me a token for good, that they who hate me may see it and be ashamed.' (*Psalm* 76:17.) DAVID said to God, after his sin with *Bathsheba* (*Samuel* 2), 'Sovereign of the Universe, pardon me for my sin.' The Lord answered, 'I will pardon thee.' Then said DAVID, 'Show me the token in my lifetime,' but God said, 'Not in thy lifetime, but in the lifetime of SOLOMON, thy son, will I show it.' Thus, when SOLOMON dedicated the temple, though he prayed with fervent devotion, he was not answered until he said, 'O Lord God, turn not away from the face of thy anointed. Remember the pious deeds of DAVID, thy servant.' (2 *Chron.* 6:42.) Then he was speedily answered, for in the next verse we read, 'And when SOLOMON had made an end of praying, a fire came down from Heaven and consumed the burnt offering and the sacrifices, and the glory of the Lord filled the house.' Then were the enemies of DAVID put to shame, for all *Israel* knew that God had pardoned DAVID for his sin. Did not SOLOMON say well then, 'Thereupon praised I the dead?' For this reason, further on in the chapter we read, 'And on the three-and-twentieth day of the seventh month he dismissed the people unto their tents, joyful and glad of heart, because of the good that the Lord had done for DAVID, and for SOLOMON, and for ISRAEL, His people.'"

SOLOMON said, "For a living dog fareth better than a dead lion."

Expounding this verse, *Rabbi Judah* said, in the name of *Rab,* "What is the meaning of the verse, 'Let me know, O Lord, my end, and the measure of my days, what it is; I wish to know when I shall cease to be.' (*Psalm* 39:5.)

"David said to God, 'Let me know, O Lord, my end.' God answered, 'I have decreed that for each one his end must be veiled in the future.' Then DAVID said, 'What is the measure of my days?' Again God replied, 'No man may know the measure of his days.' 'I wish to know when I shall cease to be,' continued DAVID; and God answered, 'Thou wilt die on a Sabbath.'

"'Let me die the day after,' entreated DAVID, but the Lord answered, 'No; then the kingdom will be SOLOMON'S, and one reign may not take away from another reign even so much as a hair's breadth.' 'Then let me die the day before,' exclaimed DAVID, 'for a day in Thy courts is better than a thousand elsewhere,' and God said, 'One day spent by thee in studying my law is more acceptable than the thousand burnt offerings thy son SOLOMON will sacrifice.'

"It was DAVID's custom to pass every Sabbath in the study of the Bible and its precepts, and he was thus engaged upon the Sabbath which was to be his last. Back of the king's palace there was an orchard, and DAVID, hearing a noise therein, walked thither to ascertain its cause. On entering the orchard he fell to the ground, dead.

"The noise in the orchard had been caused by the barking of the king's dogs, who had not that day received their food. SOLOMON sent a message to the Rabbinical College, saying, 'My father lies dead in his orchard; is it allowable to remove his body on the Sabbath? The dogs of my father are entreating for their food; is it proper to cut meat for them today?' This answer was returned by the college: 'Thy father's body should not be removed today, but give meat to the dogs.' Therefore said SOLOMON, 'A living dog fareth better than a dead lion,' justly comparing the son of *Jesse* to that king of beasts."

SOLOMON was the chosen of the Lord, who called him, through the mouth of *Nathan*, the prophet, *Yedidiah* (the beloved one). He was called SOLOMON (peace), because in his days peace reigned, as it is written, "And *Judah* and *Israel* dwelt in safety." (*Kings* 5:5.) He was called *Ithiel* (God with me) because God was his support.

And when SOLOMON sat upon the throne of his father DAVID, all the nations of the earth feared him; all the people of the earth listened anxiously for his words of wisdom.

Afterwards he had a throne made especially for himself by *Hiram*, the son of a widow of *Tyre*. It was covered with gold of *Ophir*, set with all kinds of precious and valuable stones. The seat of the throne was approached by six broad steps. The right side of the first step was guarded by an ox made of pure gold, and the left side by a lion of the same metal. On the right of the second step stood a bear also of gold, and upon the left a lamb, symbolical of enemies dwelling in peace together. On the right of the third step was placed a golden camel, and on the left an eagle. On the right of the fourth step there was also an eagle with outspread wings, and on the left a bird of prey, all of the same precious metal. On the fifth step to the right a golden cat crouching in position; on the left a chicken. On the right of the sixth step a hawk was fashioned, and on the left side a pigeon, and upon the top of the step a pigeon clutched a hawk in her talons. These animals were designed to typify the time when those of adverse natures shall unite in harmony, as it is written in *Isaiah* (11:6), "And the wolf shall then dwell with the sheep."

Over the throne was hung a chandelier of gold with seven branches; it was ornamented with roses, knobs, bowls, and tongs; and on the seven branches the names of the seven patriarchs, *Adam, Noah, Shem, Abraham, Isaac, Jacob*, and *Job*, were engraven.

On the second row of the branches of the chandelier were engraven the names of the seven pious ones of the world, *Levi*, *Kehath*, *Amram*, *Moses*, *Aaron*, *Eldad*, and *Madad*. Above all this hung a golden churn filled with pure olive oil, and on this was engraven the names of *Eli*, the *High Priest*, and his two sons, *Hophni* and *Phineas*, and on the other side the names of the two sons of *Aaron*, *Nadab* and *Abihu*.

On the right hand of the throne two chairs were placed, one for the *High Priest*, and the other for the *Vice-High Priest*, and upon the left side, from the top to the ground, seventy-one chairs were stationed as seats for the members of the *Sanhedrim*.

The throne was made upon wheels, that it could be moved easily wherever the king might desire it to be.

The Lord gave SOLOMON the power of understanding the nature and properties of the herbs of the field and the trees of the forest, as it is written, "And he spoke concerning the trees, from the cedar tree that is upon the *Lebanon* even unto the hyssop that springeth out of the wall. He spoke also concerning the beasts, and concerning the fowls, and concerning the creeping things, and concerning the fishes." (1 *Kings* 5:13.)

It is said that SOLOMON ruled the whole world, and this verse is quoted as proof of the assertion, "And SOLOMON was ruling over all the kingdoms, which brought presents, and served SOLOMON all the days of his life." (1 *Kings* 5:1.)

All the kingdoms congratulated SOLOMON as the worthy successor of his father, DAVID, whose fame was great among the nations; all save one, the kingdom of *Sheba*, the capital of which was called *Kitore*.

To this kingdom SOLOMON sent a letter:

"From me, King SOLOMON, peace to thee and to thy government. Let it be known to thee that the Almighty God has made me to reign over the whole world, the kingdoms of the *North*, the *South*, the *East*, and the *West*. Lo, they have come to me with their congratulations, all save thee alone.

"Come thou also, I pray thee, and submit to my authority, and much honour shall be done thee; but if thou refusest, behold, I shall by force compel thy acknowledgment.

"To thee *Queen Sheba*, is addressed this letter in peace from me, King SOLOMON, the son of DAVID."

Now when *Queen Sheba* received this letter, she sent in haste for her elders and counsellors to ask their advice as to the nature of her reply.

They spoke but lightly of the message and the one who sent it, but the queen did not regard their words. She sent a vessel, carrying many presents of different metals, minerals, and precious stones, to SOLOMON. It was after a voyage of two years' time that these presents arrived at *Jerusalem*, and in a letter intrusted to the captain the queen said, "After thou hast received the message then I myself will come to thee." And in two years after this time *Queen Sheba* arrived at *Jerusalem.*

When SOLOMON heard that the queen was coming he sent *Benayahu,* the son of *Yehoyadah,* the general of his army, to meet her. When the queen saw him she thought he was the king, and she alighted from her carriage.

Then *Benayahu* asked, "Why alightest thou from thy carriage?" And she answered, "Art thou not his majesty, the king?"

"No," replied *Benayahu,* "I am but one of his officers."

Then the queen turned back and said to her ladies in attendance, "If this is but one of the officers, and he is so noble and imposing in appearance, how great must be his superior, the king."

And *Benayahu,* the son of *Yehoyadah,* conducted *Queen Sheba* to the palace of the king.

SOLOMON prepared to receive his visitor in an apartment laid and lined with glass, and the queen at first was so deceived by the appearance that she imagined the king to be sitting in water.

And when the queen had tested SOLOMON's wisdom, and witnessed his magnificence, she said:

"I believed not what I heard, but now I have come, and my eyes have seen it all; behold, the half has not been told to me. Happy are thy servants who stand before thee continually to listen to thy words of wisdom. Blessed be the Lord thy God, who hath placed thee on a throne to rule righteously and in justice."

When other kingdoms heard the words of the *Queen of Sheba* they feared SOLOMON exceedingly, and he became greater than all the other kings of the earth in wisdom and in wealth.

SOLOMON was born in the year 2912 A.M., and reigned over *Israel* forty years. Four hundred and thirty-three years elapsed between the date of Solomon's reign and that of the *Temple's* destruction.

PLATE 1.

Fig. 1.

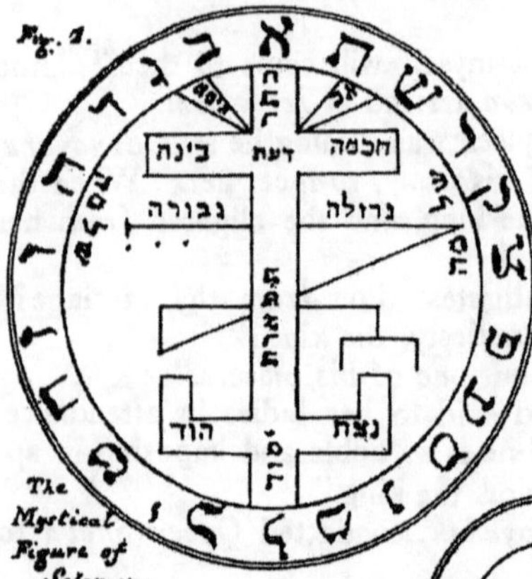

The Mystical Figure of Solomon.

Fig. 3.

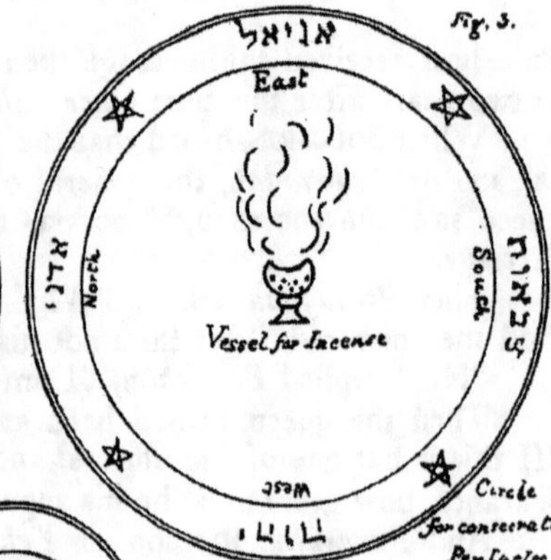

Circle for consecrating Pentacles &c.

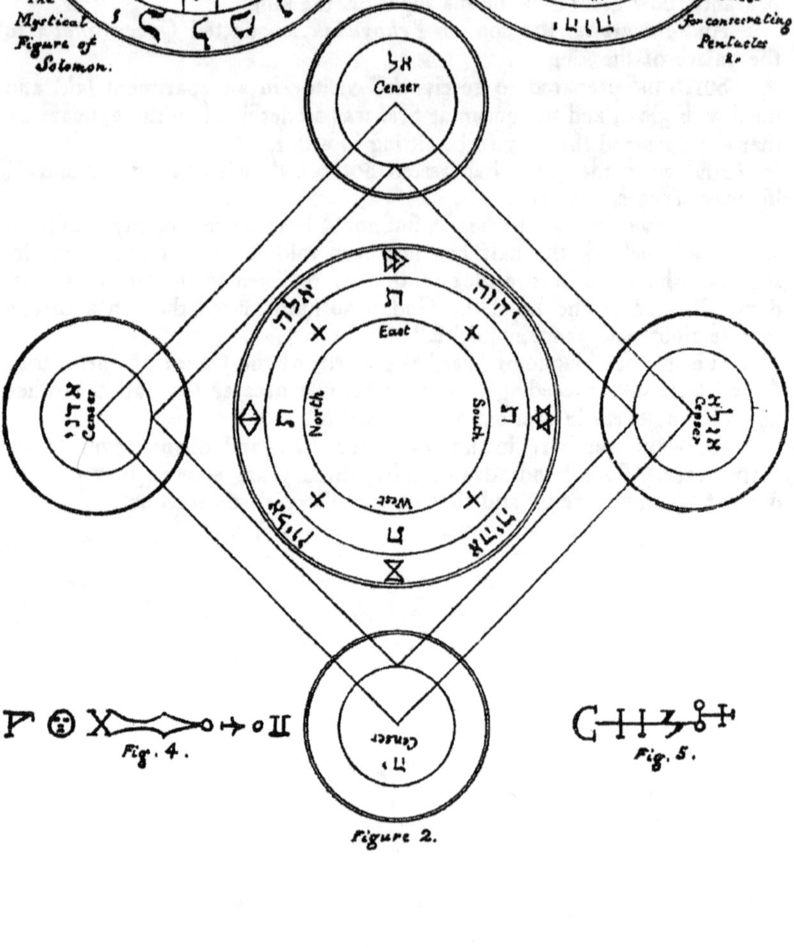

Fig. 4.

Fig. 5.

Figure 2.

INTRODUCTION.

From Add. MSS. 10862, "*The Key of Solomon,*" *translated into Latin from the Hebrew idiom.*

TREASURE up, O my son Roboam! the wisdom of my words, seeing that I SOLOMON, have received it from the Lord.

Then answered Roboam, and said: How have I deserved to follow the example of of my father SOLOMON in such things, who hath been found worthy to receive the knowledge of all living things through (the teaching of) an Angel of God?

And SOLOMON said: Hear, O my son, and receive my sayings, and learn the wonders of God. For, on a certain night, when I laid me down to sleep, I called upon that most holy Name of God, IAH, and prayed for the *Ineffable Wisdom,* and when I was beginning to close mine eyes, the Angel of the Lord, even *Homadiel,* appeared unto me, spake many things courteously unto me, and said: Listen O SOLOMON! thy prayer before the Most High is not in vain, and since thou hast asked neither for long life, nor for much riches, nor for the souls of thine enemies, but hast asked for thyself wisdom to perform justice. Thus saith the Lord: According to thy word have I given unto thee a wise and understanding heart, so that before thee was none like unto thee, nor ever shall arise.

And when I comprehended the speech which was made unto me, I understood that in me was the knowledge of all creatures, both things which are in the heavens and things which are beneath the heavens; and I saw that all the writings and wisdom of this present age were vain and futile, and that no man was perfect. And I composed a certain work wherein I rehearsed the secret of secrets, in which I have preserved them hidden, and I have also therein concealed all secrets whatsoever of magical arts of any masters; any secret or experiments, namely, of these sciences which is in any way worth being accomplished. Also I have written them in this "*Key,*" so that like as a key openeth a treasure-house, so this *Key* alone may open the knowledge and understanding of *magical arts* and sciences.

Therefore, O my son! thou mayest see every experiment of mine or of others, and let everything be properly prepared for them, as thou shalt see properly set down by me, both day and hour, and all things necessary; for without this there will be but falsehood and vanity in this my work; wherein are hidden all secrets and mysteries which can be performed; and that which is (set down) concerning a single divination or a single experiment, that same I think concerning all things which are in the Universe, and which have been, and which shall be in future time.

Therefore, O my son Roboam, I command thee by the blessing which thou expectest from thy father, that thou shall make an *Ivory Casket,* and therein place, keep, and hide this my "*Key*"; and when I shall have passed away unto my fathers, I entreat thee to place the same in my *Sepulchre* beside me, lest at another time it might fall into the hands of the wicked. And as SOLOMON commanded, so was it done.

And when, therefore (men) had waited for a long time, there came unto the *Sepulchre* certain *Babylonian Philosophers;* and when they had assembled they at once took counsel together that a certain number of men should renew the *Sepulchre* in his (SOLOMON'S) honour; and when the *Sepulchre* was dug out and repaired the *Ivory Casket* was discovered, and therein was the *Key of Secrets,* which they took with joyful mind, and when they had opened it none among them could understand it on account of the obscurity of the words and their *Occult* arrangement, and the hidden character of the sense and knowledge, for they were not worthy to possess this treasure.

Then, therefore, arose one among them, more worthy (than the others), both in the sight of the gods, and by reason of his age, who was called *Iohé Grevis,* and said unto the others: Unless we shall come and ask the interpretation from the Lord, with tears and entreaties, we shall never arrive at the knowledge of it.

Therefore, when each of them had retired to his bed, *Iohé* indeed falling upon his face on the earth, began to weep, and striking his breast, and:

What have I deserved (above others), seeing that so many men can neither understand nor interpret this knowledge, even though there were no secret thing in nature which the Lord hath hidden from me! Wherefore are these words so obscure? Wherefore am I so ignorant?

And then on his bended knees, stretching his hands to Heaven, he said:

O God, the Creator of all, Thou Who knowest all things, Who gavest so great Wisdom unto SOLOMON THE SON OF DAVID THE KING; grant unto me, I beseech Thee, O Holy Omnipotent and Ineffable Father, to receive the virtue of that wisdom, so that I may become worthy by Thine aid to attain unto the understanding of this *Key Of Secrets.*

And immediately there appeared unto me, the Angel of the Lord, saying:

Do thou remember if the secrets of SOLOMON appear hidden and obscure unto thee, that the Lord hath wished it, so that such wisdom may not fall into the hands of wicked men; wherefore do thou promise unto me, that thou art not willing that so great wisdom should ever come to any living creature, and that which thou revealest unto any let them know that they must keep it unto themselves, otherwise the secrets are profaned and no effect can follow?

And *Iohé* answered: I promise unto thee that to none will I reveal (them), save to the honour of the Lord, and with much discipline, unto peninent, secret, and faithful (persons).

Then answered the Angel: Go and read the "*Key,*" and its words which were obscure throughout shall be manifest unto thee.

And after this the Angel ascended into Heaven in a Flame of Fire.

Then *Iohé* was glad, and labouring with a clear mind, understood that which the Angel of the Lord had said, and he saw that THE KEY OF SOLOMON was changed, so that it appeared quite clear unto him plainly in all parts. And *Iohé* understood that this Work might fall into the hands of the ignorant, and he said: I conjure him into whose hands this secret may come, by the Power of the Creator, and His Wisdom, that in all things he may, desire, intend and perform, that this Treasure may come unto no unworthy (person), nor may he manifest it unto any who is unwise, nor unto one who feareth not God. Because if he act otherwise, I pray God that he may never be worthy to attain unto the desired effect.

And so he deposited the *"Key,"* which SOLOMON preserved, in the *Ivory Casket.* But the Words of the *"Key"* are as follows, divided into TWO BOOKS, and shown in order.

AN ADMONISHMENT BY de LAURENCE.

In presenting to the student of *Occultism* this translation from a most ancient and historical *Manuscript,* now in the *British Museum,* London, an admonishment is necessary.

For the space of twenty years, the writer has had many hundreds of urgent requests from serious investigators and advanced *Occult* students for an authentic and official copy of *"The Key of* SOLOMON, *Son of David, King of Israel."* Of these students, those who have made this request, are that class which are intensely interested in the production of such *Seals* and *Charms* as are used in different operations and experiments. I shall, however, admonish the one who reads here that if he would succeed, in these things, and have his wish gratified, by being able to perform these operations, it will be absolutely necessary for him to previously arrange all things which are essential, and to observe and practice the instructions contained herein.

To be brief, it will be necessary for the *Disciple* to prescribe care and observation, to abstain from all things unlawful, and from every kind of impiety. Again, the *Disciple* should put into practice the operations as they are set down herein. Therefore, let it be understood that there is nothing further to add to the instructions contained herein, as all the information that was contained in *King* SOLOMON'S *Manuscripts* is included in this *Volume.* Let the students study it seriously and with proper meditation, and he will have his mind enlightened and advance by degrees; but under no circumstances can he expect to go forward without serious study and deep meditation. Let the one who reads here realize that to learn the work of the Old Masters, and such great men as SOLOMON, who, in his time, became *King Of Israel,* is no slight task and requires faithful application.

From Lansdowne MSS. 1203, *"The Veritable Clavicles of Solomon," translated from the Hebrew into the Latin by the Rabbi Abognazar.*

O my Son Roboam! seeing that of all Sciences there is none more useful than the knowledge of *Celestial Movements,* I have thought it my duty, being at the point of death, to leave thee an inheritance more precious than all the riches which I have enjoyed. And in order that thou mayest understand how I have arrived at this degree (of wisdom), it is necessary to tell thee that one day, when I was meditating upon the power of the *Supreme Being,* the Angel of the great God appeared before me as I was saying, O how wonderful are the works of God! I suddenly beheld, at the end of a thickly-shaded vista of trees, a Light in the form of a blazing *Star,* which said unto me with a voice of thunder: SOLOMON, SOLOMON, be not dismayed; the Lord is willing to satisfy thy desire by giving thee knowledge of whatsoever thing is most pleasant unto thee. I order thee to ask of Him whatsoever thou desirest. Whereupon, recovering from my surprise, I answered unto the Angel, that according to the Will of the Lord, I only desired the Gift of Wisdom, and by the Grace of God I obtained in addition the enjoyment of all the *Celestial* treasures and the knowledge of all natural things.

It is by this means, my Son, that I possess all the virtues and riches of which thou now seest me in the enjoyment, and in order that thou mayest be willing to be attentive to all which I am about to relate to thee, and that thou mayest retain with care all that I am about to tell thee, I assure thee that the Graces of the Great God will be familiar unto thee, and that the *Celestial* and *Terrestrial Creatures* will be obedient unto thee, and a science which only works by the strength and power of natural things, and by the pure Angels which govern them. Of which latter I will give thee the names in order, their exercises and particular employments to which they are destined, together with the days over which they particularly preside, in order that thou mayest arrive at the accomplishment of all, which thou wilt find in this my *Testament.* In all which I promise thee success, provided that all thy works only tend unto the honour of God, Who hath given me the power to rule, not only over *Terrestrial* but also over *Celestial* things, that is to say, over the Angels, of whom I am able to dispose according to my will, and to obtain from them very considerable services.

Firstly. It is necessary for thee to understand that God, having made all things, in order that they may be submitted unto Him, hath wished to bring His works to perfection, by making one which participates of the Divine and of the *Terrestrial,* that is to say, Man; whose body is gross and terrestrial, while his soul is spiritual and celestial, unto whom He hath made subject the whole earth and its inhabitants, and hath given unto Him means by which He may render the Angels familiar, as I call those *Celestial* creatures who are destined: some to regulate the motion of the Stars, others to inhabit the Elements, others to aid and direct men, and others again to sing continually the praises of the Lord. Thou mayest then, by the use of their *Seals* and *Characters,* render them familiar unto thee, provided that thou abusest not this privilege by demanding from them things which are contrary to their nature; for accursed be he who will take the Name of God in vain, and who will employ for evil purposes the knowledge and good wherewith He hath enriched us.

I command thee, my Son, to carefully engrave in thy memory all that I say unto thee, in order that it may never leave thee. If thou dost not intend to use for a good purpose the secrets which I here teach thee, I command thee rather to cast this Testament into the fire, than to abuse the power thou wilt have of constraining the Spirits, for I warn thee that the beneficent Angels, wearied and fatigued by thine illicit demands, would to thy sorrow execute the commands of God, as well as to that of all such who, with evil intent, would abuse those secrets which He hath given and revealed unto me. Think not, however, O my Son, that it would not be permitted thee to profit by the good fortune and happiness which the Divine Spirits can bring thee; on the contrary, it gives them great pleasure to render service to Man for whom many of these Spirits have great liking and affinity, God having destined them for the preservation and guidance of those Terrestrial things which are submitted to the power of Man.*

There are different kinds of Spirits, according to the things over which they preside, some of them govern the *Empyrean Heaven,* others the *Primum Mobilé,* others the *First* and *Second Crystalline,* others the *Starry Heaven;* there are also Spirits of the *Heaven of Saturn,* which I call *Saturnites;* there are Jovial, Martial, Solar, Venerean, Mercurial, and Lunar Spirits; there are also (Spirits) in the Elements as well as in the Heavens, there are some in the Fiery Region, others in the Air, others in the Water, and others upon the Earth, which can all render service to that man who learns their nature, and knows how to attract them.

Furthermore, I wish to make thee understand that God hath destined to each one of us a Spirit, which watches over us and takes care of our preservation; these are called *Genii,* who are elementary like us, and who are more ready to render service to those whose temperament is conformed to the Element which these *Genii* inhabit; for example, shouldest thou be of a fiery temperament, that is to say sanguine, thy genius would be fiery and submitted to the *Empire of Baël.* Besides this, there are special times reserved for the invocation of these Spirits, in the days and hours when they have power and absolute empire. It is for this reason that thou wilt see in the following tables to what Planet and to what Angel each Day and Hour is submitted, together with the Colours which belong unto them, the Metals, Herbs, Plants, Aquatic, Aërial, and Terrestrial Animals, and *Temple Incense,* which are proper to each of them, as also in what quarter of the Universe they ask to be invoked. Neither are omitted, the *Conjurations, Seals, Characters,* and *Divine Letters,* which belong to them, by means of which we receive the power to sympathize with these Spirits.

* The Disciple must pay strict attention to this command.

Sunday.	*Monday.*	*Tuesday.*	*Wednes.*	*Hours from Sunset to Sunset.*	*Hours from Midnight to Midnight.*	*Thursd.*	*Friday.*	*Saturd.*
Merc.	Jup.	Ven.	Sat.	8	1	Sun.	Moon.	Mars.
Moon.	Mars.	Mer.	Jup.	9	2	Ven.	Sat.	Sun.
Sat.	Sun.	Moon.	Mars.	10	3	Mer.	Jup.	Ven.
Jup.	Ven.	Sat.	Sun	11	4	Moon.	Mars.	Mer.
Mars.	Mer.	Jup.	Ven.	12	5	Sat.	Sun.	Moon.
Sun.	Moon.	Mars.	Mer.	1	6	Jup.	Ven.	Sat.
Ven.	Sat.	Sun.	Moon.	2	7	Mars.	Mer.	Jup.
Mer.	Jup.	Ven.	Sat.	3	8	Sun.	Moon.	Mars.
Moon.	Mars.	Mer.	Jup.	4	9	Ven.	Sat.	Sun.
Sat.	Sun.	Moon.	Mars.	5	10	Mer.	Jup.	Ven.
Jup.	Ven.	Sat.	Sun.	6	11	Moon.	Mars.	Mer.
Mars.	Mer.	Jup.	Ven.	7	12	Sat.	Sun.	Moon.
Sun.	Moon.	Mars.	Mer.	8	1	Jup.	Ven.	Sat.
Ven.	Sat.	Sun.	Moon.	9	2	Mars.	Mer.	Jup.
Mer.	Jup.	Ven.	Sat.	10	3	Sun.	Moon.	Mars.
Moon.	Mars.	Mer.	Jup.	11	4	Ven.	Sat.	Sun.
Sat.	Sun.	Moon.	Mars.	12	5	Mer.	Jup.	Ven.
Jup.	Ven.	Sat.	Sun.	1	6	Moon.	Mars.	Mer.
Mars.	Mer.	Jup.	Ven.	2	7	Sat.	Sun.	Moon.
Sun.	Moon.	Mars.	Mer.	3	8	Jup.	Ven.	Sat.
Ven.	Sat.	Sun.	Moon.	4	9	Mars.	Mer.	Jup.
Mer.	Jup.	Ven.	Sat.	5	10	Sun.	Moon.	Mars.
Moon.	Mars.	Mer.	Jup.	6	11	Ven.	Sat.	Sun.
Sat.	Sun.	Moon.	Mars.	7	12	Mer.	Jup.	Ven.

Table of the Magical Names of the Hours, and of the Angels who rule them, commencing at the first hour after Midnight of each day, and ending at the ensuing midnight.

Hours.	*Sunday.*	*Monday.*	*Tuesday.*	*Wednesd.*	*Thursd.*	*Friday.*	*Saturday.*
1. Yayn . . .	Raphael	Sachiel	Anael	Cassiel	Michael	Gabriel	Zamael
2. Yanor . .	Gabriel	Zamael	Raphael	Sachiel	Anael	Cassiel	Michael
3. Nasnia . .	Cassiel	Michael	Gabriel	Zamael	Raphael	Sachiel	Anael
4. Salla . . .	Sachiel	Anael	Cassiel	Michael	Gabriel	Zamael	Raphael
5. Sadedali . .	Zamael	Raphael	Sachiel	Anael	Cassiel	Michael	Gabriel
6. Thamur . .	Michael	Gabriel	Zamael	Raphael	Sachiel	Anael	Cassiel
7. Ourer . .	Anael	Cassiel	Michael	Gabriel	Zamael	Raphael	Sachiel
8. Thainé . .	Raphael	Sachiel	Anael	Cassiel	Michael	Gabriel	Zamael
9. Neron . .	Gabriel	Zamael	Raphael	Sachiel	Anael	Cassiel	Michael
10. Yayon . .	Cassiel	Michael	Gabriel	Zamael	Raphael	Sachiel	Anael
11. Abai . . .	Sachiel	Anael	Cassiel	Michael	Gabriel	Zamael	Raphael
12. Nathalon .	Zamael	Raphael	Sachiel	Anael	Cassiel	Michael	Gabriel
1. Beron . .	Michael	Gabriel	Zamael	Raphael	Sachiel	Anael	Cassiel
2. Barol . .	Anael	Cassiel	Michael	Gabriel	Zamael	Raphael	Sachiel
3. Thanu . .	Raphael	Sachiel	Anael	Cassiel	Michael	Gabriel	Zamael
4. Athor . .	Gabriel	Zamael	Raphael	Sachiel	Anael	Cassiel	Michael
5. Mathon . .	Cassiel	Michael	Gabriel	Zamael	Raphael	Sachiel	Anael
6. Rana . .	Sachiel	Anael	Cassiel	Michael	Gabriel	Zamael	Raphael
7. Netos . .	Zamael	Raphael	Sachiel	Anael	Cassiel	Michael	Gabriel
8. Tafrac . .	Michael	Gabriel	Zamael	Raphael	Sachiel	Anael	Cassiel
9. Sassur . .	Anael	Cassiel	Michael	Gabriel	Zamael	Raphael	Sachiel
10. Agla . . .	Raphael	Sachiel	Anael	Cassiel	Michael	Gabriel	Zamael
11. Cäerra . .	Gabriel	Zamael	Raphael	Sachiel	Anael	Cassiel	Michael
12. Salam . .	Cassiel	Michael	Gabriel	Zamael	Raphael	Sachiel	Anael

Table of the Archangels, Angels, Metals, Days of the Week, and Colours Attributed to each Planet.

Days.	*Saturday.*	*Thursd.*	*Tuesday.*	*Sunday*	*Friday.*	*Wednesd.*	*Monday.*
Archangel . .	Tzaphqiel	Tzadiqel	Khamael	Raphael	Haniel	Michael	Gabriel
Angel . . .	Cassiel	Sachiel	Zamael	Michael	Anael	Raphael	Gabriel
Planet . . .	Saturn	Jupiter	Mars	Sun	Venus	Mercury	Moon
Metal. . . .	Lead	Tin	Iron	Gold	Copper	Mercury	Silver
Colour . . .	Black	Blue	Red	Yellow	Green	Purple or Mixed Colours	White

NOTE BY de LAURENCE.

These *Tables* have been *collated* and compared with various examples of both MS. and printed. They are to be used thus:—Supposing the student wishes to discover the properties of the hour from 12 to 1 o'clock p.m. on a Tuesday, let him look in the "*Table of the Planetary Hours,*" and having found the hour marked 1 in the column headed "*Hours from Midnight to Midnight,*" he will see in the column headed "*Hours from Sunset to Sunset,*" on the same line the figure 8, showing it to be the eighth hour of the day; and in the column headed Tuesday, the name Mars, showing that it is under the dominion of the planet Mars. On consulting the "*Table of the Magical Names of the Hours,*" &c., he will find under the number 1, the name *Beron,* and in the column "Tuesday," the name of the angel *Zamael* over against it on the same line, showing that the ruler of the hour is the Angel Zamael, and that its Magical Name is *Beron.* Further, on referring to the third Table he will see that Tuesday is under the rule of the planet Mars, whose Archangel is *Khamael, Angel Zamael, Metal Iron, and Colour Red.* Similarly it will be found that the hour from 10 to 11 p.m. on Saturday is the sixth hour of the night, under the dominion of the Sun, that its Magical Name is *Cäerra,* and that the *Angel Michael* rules it; while Saturday itself is under the dominion of the *Archangel Tzaphqiel,* of the *Angel Cassiel,* of the *Planet Saturn,* and that the *Metal Lead* and the *Colour Black* are applicable to it.

The ensuing Text is taken from the following MSS., collated and compared with each other.

Sloane MSS. 1307; *Sloane* MSS. 3091; *Harleian* MSS. 3981; *Add.* MSS. 10862; *King's* MSS. 288; *Lansdowne* MSS. 1202.

Extracts have also been made from *Lansdowne* MSS. 1203, which differs considerably from the others in general arrangement, though containing very similar matter.

In cases where the MSS. varied from each other I have taken the version which seemed most likely to be correct, in some cases mentioning the variant readings in footnotes. I have also corrected the Hebrew names in the Incantations, for these were in some cases so marred as to be hardly recognisable; e.g. *Zenard,* written for *Tzabaoth,* &c.

PRELIMINARY DISCOURSE.

From Lansdowne MSS. 1203, "The Veritable Clavicles of Solomon," translated from the Hebrew into the Latin language by the Rabbi Abognazar.

EVERY one knoweth in the present day that from time immemorial SOLOMON possessed knowledge inspired by the wise teachings of an angel,* to which he appeared so submissive and obedient, that in addition to the gift of wisdom, which he demanded, he obtained with profusion all the other virtues; which happened in order that knowledge worthy of eternal preservation might not be buried with his body. Being, so to speak, near his end, he left to his son *Roboam* a Testament which should contain all (the Wisdom) he had possessed prior to his death. The *Rabbins,* who were careful to cultivate (the same knowledge) after him, called this Testament *"The Clavicle, or Key of Solomon,"* which they caused to be engraved on (pieces of) the bark of trees, while the *Pentacles* were inscribed in Hebrew letters on plates of copper, so that they might be carefully preserved in the *Temple* which that wise king had caused to be built.

This Testament was in ancient time translated from the Hebrew into the Latin language by *Rabbi Abognazar,* who transported it with him into the town of Arles in Provence, where by a notable piece of good fortune the ancient *Hebrew Clavicle,* that is to say, this precious translation of it, fell into the hands of the Archbishop of Arles, after the destruction of the Jews in that city; who, from the Latin, translated it into the vulgar tongue, in the same terms which here follow, without having either changed or augmented the original translation from the Hebrew.

* An angel, is, today known as a good helpful spirit on the Astral Plane. In Solomon's time they were called angels or devils. Today they are spoken of as good or evil spirits or influences.—EDITOR'S NOTE.

The Key Of Solomon.

(CLAVICULA SALOMONIS.)

The Beginning Of Book One.

CHAPTER I.

Concerning the Divine Love Which Precedes the Acquisition of This Knowledge.

Solomon, the Son of David, King of Israel, hath said that the beginning of our Key is to fear God, to adore Him, to honour Him with contrition of heart, to invoke Him* in all matters which we wish to undertake, and to operate with very great devotion, for thus God will lead us in the right way. When, therefore, thou shalt wish to acquire the knowledge of Magical Arts and Sciences, it is necessary to have prepared the order of hours and of days, and of the position of the Moon, without the operation of which thou canst effect nothing; but if thou observest them with diligence thou mayest easily and thoroughly arrive at the effect and end which thou desirest to attain.

* 1202, Lansdowne MSS., omits the concluding part of this sentence.

BOOK ONE.

CHAPTER II.

Of the Days, and Hours, and of the Virtues of the Planets.

When* thou wishest to make any experiment or operation, thou must first prepare, beforehand, all the requisites, such as candles and Incense,† which thou wilt find described in the following Chapters: observing the days, the hours, and the other effects of the Constellations which may be found in this Chapter.

It is, therefore, advisable to know that the hours of the day and of the night together, are twenty-four in number, and that each hour is governed by one of the Seven Planets in regular order, commencing at the highest and descending to the lowest. The order of the Planets is as follows: ShBThAI, Shabbathai, Saturn; beneath Saturn is TzDQ, Tzedeq, Jupiter; beneath Jupiter is MADIM, Madim, Mars; beneath Mars is ShMSh, Shemesh, the Sun; beneath the Sun is NVGH, Nogah, Venus; beneath Venus is KVKB, Kokav, Mercury; and beneath Mercury is LBNH, Levanah, the Moon, which is the lowest of all the Planets.

It must, therefore, be understood that the Planets have their dominion over the day which approacheth nearest unto the name which is given and attributed unto them—viz., over Saturday, Saturn; Thursday, Jupiter; Tuesday, Mars; Sunday, the Sun; Friday, Venus; Wednesday, Mercury; and Monday, the Moon.

The rule of the Planets over each hour begins from the dawn at the rising of the Sun on the day which take its name from such Planet, and the Planet which follows it in order, succeeds to the rule over the next hour. Thus (on Saturday) Saturn rules the first hour, Jupiter the Second, Mars the third, the Sun the fourth, Venus the fifth, Mercury the sixth, the Moon the seventh, and Saturn returns in the rule over the eighth, and the others in their turn, the Planets always keeping the same relative order.

Note that each experiment or magical operation should be performed under the Planet, and usually in the hour, which refers to the same. For example:—

In the Days and Hours of Saturn thou canst perform experiments to summon the Souls from Hades, but only of those who have died a natural death. Similarly on these days and hours thou canst operate to bring either good or bad fortune to buildings; to have familiar Spirits attend thee in sleep; to cause good or ill success to business, possessions, goods, seeds,

* This first paragraph is omitted in 1307 Sloane MSS., and in 10862 Add. MSS.

† Those who wish a supply of Temple Incense or Candles will find the very same listed in Messrs. de Laurence, Scott & Co.'s great Occult Book Catalogue.

fruits, and similar things, in order to acquire learning; to bring destruction and to give death, and to sow hatred and discord.

The Days and Hours of Jupiter are proper for obtaining honours, acquiring riches; contracting friendships, preserving health; and arriving at all that thou canst desire.

In the Days and Hours of Mars thou canst make experiments regarding War; to arrive at military honour; to acquire courage; to overthrow enemies; and further to cause ruin, slaughter, cruelty, discord; to wound and to give death.

The Days and Hours of the Sun are very good for perfecting experiments regarding temporal wealth, hope, gain, fortune, divination, the favour of princes, to dissolve hostile feeling, and to make friends.

The Days and Hours of Venus are good for forming friendships; for kindness and love; for joyous and pleasant undertakings, and for traveling.

The Days and Hours of Mercury are good to operate for eloquence and intelligence; promptitude in business; science and divination; wonders; apparitions; and answers regarding the future. Thou canst also operate under this Planet for thefts; writings; deceit; and merchandise.

The Days and Hours of the Moon are good for embassies; voyages; envoys; messages; navigation; reconciliation; love; and the acquisition of merchandise by water.*

Thou shouldest take care punctually to observe all the instructions contained in this chapter, if thou desirest to succeed, seeing that the truth of Magical Science dependeth thereon.

The Hours of Saturn, of Mars, and of the Moon are alike good for communicating and speaking with Spirits; as those of Mercury are for recovering thefts by the means of Spirits.

The Hours of Mars serve for summoning Souls from Hades,† especially of those slain in battle.

The Hours of the Sun, of Jupiter, and of Venus, are adapted for preparing any operations whatsoever of love, of kindness, and of invisibility, as is hereafter more fully shown, to which must be added other things of a similar nature which are contained in our work.

The Hours of Saturn and Mars and also the days on which the Moon is conjunct‡ with them, or when she receives their opposition or quartile aspect, are excellent for making experiments of hatred, enmity, quarrel, and discord; and other operations of the same kind which are given later on in this work.

* Much of these foregoing instructions is omitted in the 10862 Add. MSS., but given in a different way in the ensuing paragraphs.

† In the French "des Enfers," in the Latin "Inferis."

‡ Conjunction means being in the same degree of the Zodiac; opposition is being 180 degrees, and quartile 90 degrees apart from each other.

The Hours of Mercury are good for undertaking experiments relating to games, raillery, jests, sports, and the like.

The Hours of the Sun, of Jupiter, and of Venus, particularly on the days which they rule, are good for all extraordinary, uncommon, and unknown operations.

The Hours of the Moon are proper for making trial of experiments relating to recovery of stolen property, for obtaining nocturnal visions, for summoning Spirits in sleep, and for preparing anything relating to Water.

The Hours of Venus are furthermore useful for lots, poisons, all things of the nature of Venus, for preparing powders provocative of madness; and the like things.

But in order to thoroughly effect the operations of this Art, thou shouldest perform them not only on the Hours but on the Days of the Planets as well, because then the experiment will always succeed better, provided thou observest the rules laid down later on, for if thou omittest one single condition thou wilt never arrive at the accomplishment of the Art.

For those matters then which appertain unto the Moon, such as the Invocation of Spirit, the *Works of Necromancy,* and the recovery of stolen property, it is necessary that the Moon should be in a Terrestrial Sign, viz.:—Taurus, Virgo, or Capricorn.

For love, grace, and invisibility, the Moon should be in a Fiery Sign, viz.:—Aries, Leo, or Sagittarius.

For hatred, discord, and destruction, the Moon should be in a Watery Sign, viz.:—Cancer, Scorpio, or Pisces.

For experiments of a peculiar nature, which cannot be classed under any certain head, the Moon should be in an Airy Sign, viz.:—Gemini, Libra, or Aquarius.

But if these things seem unto thee difficult to accomplish, it will suffice thee merely to notice the Moon after her combustion, or conjunction with the Sun, especially just when she* quits his beams and appeareth visible. For then it is good to make all experiments for the construction and operation of any matter. That is why the time from the New unto the Full Moon is proper for performing any of the experiments of which we have spoken above. But in her decrease or wane it is good for War, Disturbance, and Discord. Likewise the period when she is almost deprived of light, is proper for experiments of invisibility, and of Death.

But observe inviolably that thou commence nothing while the Moon is in conjunction with the Sun, seeing that this is extremely unfortunate, and that thou wilt then be able to effect nothing; but the Moon quitting his beams and increasing in Light, thou canst perform all that thou desirest, observing nevertheless the directions in this Chapter.

Furthermore, if thou wishest to converse with Spirits it should be

* *i.e.* New Moon.

especially on the day of Mercury and in his hour, and let the Moon be in an Airy Sign,* as well as the Sun.

Retire† thou then unto a secret place, where no one may be able to see thee or to hinder thee, before the completion of the experiment, whether thou shouldest wish to work by day or by night. But if thou shouldest wish to work by night, perfect thy work on the succeeding night; if by day, seeing that the day beginneth with the rising of the Sun (perfect thy work on) the succeeding day. But the Hour of Inception is the Hour of Mercury.

Verily, since no experiments for converse with Spirits can be done without a Circle being prepared, whatsoever experiments therefore thou wishest to undertake for conversing with Spirits, therein thou must learn to construct a certain particular Circle; that being done surround that Circle with the Circle of Art for better caution and efficacy.

* In Add. MSS. 10862; "or in an Earthy Sign, as hath been before said."

† The following paragraphs to the end of this Chapter are only found in the Latin version, Add. MSS. 10862.

BOOK ONE.

CHAPTER III.

Concerning the Arts.

If thou wishest to succeed, it is necessary to make the following Experiments and Arts in the appropriate Days and Hours, with the requisite solemnities and ceremonies contained and laid down in the following chapters.

Experiments, then, are of two kinds; the first is to make trial of what, as I have said, can be easily performed without a Circle, and in this case it is not necessary to observe anything but what thou wilt find in the proper Chapters. The second can in no way be brought to perfection without the Circle; and in order to accomplish this perfectly it is necessary to take note of all the preparations which the *Master* of the Art and his *Disciples* must undertake before constructing* the Circle.

Before commencing operations both the *Master* and his *Disciples* must abstain with great and thorough continence during the space of nine days from sensual pleasures and from vain and foolish conversation; as plainly appeareth in the *Second Book, Chapter* 4. Six of these days having expired, he must recite frequently the Prayer and Confession as will be told him; and on the Seventh Day, the Master being alone, let him enter into a secret place, let him take off his clothes, and bathe himself from head to foot in consecrated and exorcised Water, saying devoutly and humbly the prayer, "O Lord Adonaï," &c., as it is written in the *Second Book, Chapter* 2.

The Prayer being finished, let the Master quit the water, and put upon his flesh raiment of white linen clean and unsoiled; and then let him go with his Disciples unto a secret place and command them to strip themselves naked; and they having taken off their clothes, let him take exorcised water and pour it upon their heads so that it flows down to their feet and bathes them completely; and while pouring this water upon them let the Master say:—*"Be ye regenerate, renewed, washed, and pure," &c., as in Book II., Chapter* 3.

Which† being done, the Disciples must clothe themselves, putting upon their flesh, like their Master, raiment of white linen clean and unsoiled; and the three last days the Master and his Disciples should fast, observing the solemnities and prayers marked in *Book II., Chapter* 2.

Note that the three last days should be calm weather, without wind, and without clouds rushing hither and thither over the face of the sky. On the last day let the Master go with his Disciples unto a secret fountain of running water, or unto a flowing stream, and there let each of them, taking off his clothes, wash himself with due solemnity, as is rehearsed

* Sloane MSS. 3091, says, "before they come to the Circle."
† This paragraph is omitted in Lansdowne MSS. 1202.

in *Book II.* And when they are clean and pure, let each put upon him garments of white linen, pure, and clean, using the prayers and ceremonies described in *Book II.* After which let the *Master* alone say the confession. The which being finished, the *Master* in sign of penitence will Kiss* the *Disciples* on the forehead, and each of them will Kiss the other. Afterwards let the *Master* extend his hands over the *Disciples*, and in sign of absolution absolve and bless them; which being done he will distribute to each of his *Disciples* the Instruments necessary for Magical Art, which he is to carry into the Circle.

The *First Disciple* will bear the *Censer*, the *Perfumes* and the *Temple Incense*,** the *Second Disciple* will bear the *Book, Papers, Pens, Ink*, and any stinking or impure materials; the *Third* will carry the *Knife* and the *Sickle of Magical Art*, the *Lantern*, and the *Candles;* the *Fourth*, the *Psalms*, and the rest of the *Instruments;* the *Fifth*, the *Crucible* or *Chafing-dish*, and the *Charcoal* or *Fuel;* but it is necessary for the Master himself to carry in his hand the *Staff*, and the *Wand* or *Rod*. The things necessary being thus disposed, the Master will go with his Disciples unto the assigned place, where they have proposed to construct the Circle for the Magical Arts and experiments; repeating on the way the prayers and orations which thou wilt find in *Book II.*

When the *Master* shall have arrived at the place appointed, together with his *Disciples*, he having lighted the flame of the fire, and having exorcised it afresh as is laid down in the *Second Book*, shall light the Candle and place it in the Lantern, which one of the *Disciples* is to hold ever in his hand to light the *Master* at his work. Now the *Master* of the Art, every time that he shall have occasion for some particular purpose to speak with the Spirits, must endeavor to form certain Circles which shall differ somewhat, and shall have some particular reference to the particular experiment under consideration. Now, in order to succeed in forming such a Circle concerning *Magical Art*, for the greater assurance and efficacy thou shalt construct it in the following manner:—

THE CONSTRUCTION OF THE CIRCLE.

Take thou the Knife, the Sickle, or the Sword of Magical Art consecrated after the manner and order which we shall deliver unto thee in the Second Book. With this Knife or with the Sickle of Art thou shalt describe, beyond the inner Circle which thou shalt have already formed, a Second Circle, encompassing the other at the distance of one foot therefrom and having the same centre.† Within this space of a foot in breadth between the first and the second circumferential‡ line, thou shalt trace towards the Four Quarters of the Earth,§ the Sacred and Venerable Sym-

* Note the "holy kiss" in the New Testament. "Greet ye one another with a holy kiss."

** Temple Incense and Special Waxen Candles can be obtained from Messrs. de Laurence, Scott & Co. by consulting their Catalogue.

† *i.e.* Two Circles enclosed between three circumferential lines.

‡ *i.e.* within the first circle.

§ *i.e.* the four Cardinal points of the compass.

bols of the holy Letter Tau.* And between the first and the second *Circle*,† which thou shalt thyself have drawn with the Instrument of *Magical Art*, thou shalt make four hexagonal pentacles,‡ and between these thou shalt write four terrible and tremendous Names of God, viz.:—

Between the East and the South the Supreme Name IHVH, *Tetragramaton*;—

Between the South and the West the Essential *Tetragrammatic* Name AHIH, Eheieh;—

Between the West and the North the Name of Power ALIVN, Elion;—

And between the North and the East the Great Name ALH, Eloah;—

Which Names are of supreme importance in the list of the Sephiroth,§ and their Sovereign Equivalents.

Furthermore, thou shalt circumscribe about these Circles two Squares, the Angles of which shall be turned towards the Four Quarters of the Earth; and the space between the Lines of the Outer and Inner Square shall be half-a-foot. The extreme Angles of the Outer Square shall be made the Centres of four Circles, the measure or diameter of which shall be one foot. All these are to be drawn with the Knife or consecrated Instrument of Art. And within these Four Circles thou must write these four Names of God the Most Holy One, in this order:—

At the East, AL, El;

At the West, IH, Yah;

At the South, AGLA, Agla;

And at the North ADNI, Adonaï.

Between the two Squares the Name *Tetragrammaton* is to be written in the same way as is shown in the plate. (*See Figure* 2.)

While constructing the Circle, the Master should recite the following Psalms:—Psalm II; Psalm LIV; Psalm CXIII; Psalm LXVII; Psalm XLVII; Psalm LXVIII.

Or he may as well recite them before tracing the Circle.

The which being finished, and the fumigations being performed, as is described in the chapter on Fumigations in the Second Book, the Master should reassemble his Disciples, encourage them, reassure them, fortify them, and conduct them into the parts of the Circle of Art, where he must place them in the four quarters of the earth, encourage them, and exhort them to fear nothing, and to keep in the places assigned to them. Also, the Disciple who is placed towards the East should have a pen, ink, paper, silk,

* The letter Tau represents the Cross, and in 10862 Add. MSS. in the drawing of the Circle, the Hebrew letter is replaced by the Cross; in 1307 Sloane MSS. by the T or Tau-Cross.

† *i.e.* in the Outer Circle, bounded by the second and third circumferential lines.

‡ 10862 Add. MSS. is the only copy which uses the word *hexagonal*, but the others show four hexagrams in the drawing; in the drawing, however, 10862 gives the hexagrams formed by various differing interlacements of two triangles, as shown in Figure 2.

§ The Sephiroth are the ten Qabalistical Emanations of the Deity. The Sovereign Equivalents are the Divine Names referred thereto.

and white cotton, all clean and suitable for the work. Furthermore, each of the Companions should have a new Sword drawn in his hand (besides the consecrated Magical Sword of Art), and he should keep his hand resting upon the hilt thereof, and he should on no pretext quit the place assigned to him, nor move therefrom.

After this the Master should quit the Circle, light the fuel in the earthen pots, and place upon them the Censers, in the Four Quarters of the Earth; and he should have in his hand the consecrated taper of wax, and he should light it and place it in a hidden and secret place prepared for it. Let him after this re-enter and close the Circle.

The *Master* should afresh exhort his *Disciples*, and explain to them all that they have to do and to observe; the which commands they should promise and vow to execute.

Let the Master then repeat this Prayer:—

PRAYER.

When we enter herein with all humility, let God the Almighty One enter into this Circle, by the entrance of an eternal happiness, of a Divine prosperity, of a perfect joy, of an abundant charity, and of an eternal salutation. Let all the demons fly from this place, especially those who are opposed unto this work, and let the Angels of Peace assist and protect this Circle, from which let discord and strife fly and depart. Magnify and extend upon us, O Lord, Thy most Holy Name, and bless our conversation and our assembly. Sanctify, O Lord our God, our humble entry herein, Thou the Blessed and Holy One of the Eternal Ages! Amen.

After this, let the Master say upon his knees, as follows:—

PRAYER.

O Lord God, All Powerful and All Merciful, Thou Who desirest not the death of a sinner, but rather that he may turn from his wickedness and live; give and grant unto us thy grace, by blessing and consecrating this earth and this circle, which is here marked out with the most powerful and holy Names of God. And thee, I conjure, O Earth, by the Most Holy Name of ASHER EHEIEH entering within this Circle, composed and made with mine hand. And may God, even ADONAI, bless this place with all the virtues of Heaven, so that no obscene or unclean spirit may have the power to enter into this Circle, or to annoy any person who is therein; though the Lord God ADONAI, Who liveth eternally unto the Ages of the Ages. Amen.

I beseech Thee, O Lord God, the All Powerful and the All Merciful, that Thou wilt deign to bless this Circle, and all this place, and all those who are therein, and that Thou wilt grant unto us, who serve Thee, and rehearse nothing but the wonders of Thy law, a good Angel for our Guardian; remove from us every adverse power; preserve us from evil and from trouble; grant, O Lord, that we may rest in this place in all safety, through Thee, O Lord, Who livest and reignest unto the Ages of the Ages. Amen.

Let the Master now arise and place upon his head a Crown made of paper (or any other appropriate substance), on the which there must be written (with the Colours and other necessary things which we shall describe hereafter), these four Names AGLA, AGLAI, AGLATA, AGLATAI. The which Names are to be placed in the front, behind, and on either side of the head.

Furthermore, the Master ought to have with him in the Circle, those Pentacles or Medals which are necessary to his purpose, which are described hereinafter, and which should be constructed according to the rules given in the Chapter on *Pentacles*. They should be described on virgin paper with a pen; and ink, blood, or colours, prepared according to the manner which we shall hereafter show in the Chapters on these subjects. It will be sufficient to take only those Pentacles which are actually required, they should be sewed to the front of the linen robe, on the chest, with the consecrated needle of the Art, and with a thread which has been woven by a young girl.

After this, let the Master turn himself towards the Eastern Quarter (unless directed to the contrary, or unless he should be wishing to call Spirits which belong to another quarter of the Universe), and pronounce with a loud voice the Conjuration contained in this Chapter. And if the Spirits be disobedient and do not then make their appearance, he must arise and take the exorcised Knife of Art wherewith he hath constructed the Circle, and raise it towards the sky as if he wished to beat or strike the Air, and conjure the Spirits. Let him then lay his right hand and the Knife upon the Pentacles or Medals, constructed of, and described upon virgin paper, which are fastened to or sewn upon his breast, and let him repeat the following Conjuration upon his knees:

CONJURATION.

O Lord, hear my prayer, and let my cry come unto Thee. O Lord God Almighty, who has reigned before the beginning of the Ages, and Who by Thine Infinite Wisdom, hast created the heavens, the earth, and the sea, and all that in them is, all that is visible, and all that is invisible by a single word; I praise Thee, I bless Thee, I adore Thee, I glorify Thee, and I pray Thee now at the present time to be merciful unto me, a miserable sinner, for I am the work of Thine hands. Save me, and direct me by Thy Holy Name, Thou to Whom nothing is difficult, nothing is impossible; and deliver me from the night of mine ignorance, and enable me to go forth therefrom. Enlighten me with a spark of Thine Infinite Wisdom. Take away from my senses the desire of covetousness, and the iniquity of mine idle words. Give unto me, Thy servant, a wise understanding, penetrating and subtle heart, to acquire and comprehend all Sciences and Arts; give unto me capacity to hear, and strength of memory to retain them, so that I may be able to accomplish my desires, and understand and learn all difficult and desirable Sciences; and also that I may be able to comprehend the hidden secrets of the Holy Writings. Give me the virtue to conceive them, so that I may be able to bring forth and pronounce my words with patience and humility, for the instruction of others, as Thou hast ordered me.

O God, the Father, All Powerful and All Merciful, Who hast created all things, Who knowest and conceivest them universally, and to Whom nothing is hidden, nothing is impossible; I entreat Thy Grace for me and for Thy servants, because Thou seest and knowest well that we perform not this work to tempt Thy Strength and Thy Power as if in doubt thereof, but rather that we may know and understand the truth of all hidden things. I beseech Thee to have the kindness to be favorable unto us; by Thy Splendour, Thy Magnificence, and Thy Holiness, and by Thy Holy, Terrible, and Ineffable Name IAH, at which the whole world doth tremble, and by the Fear with which all creatures obey Thee. Grant, O Lord, that we may become responsive unto Thy Grace, so that through it we may have a full confidence in and knowledge of Thee, and that the Spirits may discover themselves here in our presence, and that those which are gentle and peaceable may come unto us, so that they may be obedient unto Thy commands, through Thee, O Most Holy ADONAI, Whose Kingdom is an everlasting Kingdom, and Whose Empire endureth unto the Ages of the Ages. Amen.

After having said all these words devoutly, let the Master arise, and place his hands upon the Pentacles, and let one of the Companions hold the Book open before the Master, who, raising his eyes to heaven, and turning unto the Four Quarters of the Universe, shall say:

O Lord, be Thou unto me a *Tower* of *Strength* against the appearance and assault of the Evil Spirits.

After this, turning towards the Four Quarters of the Universe, he shall say the following words:—

These be the Symbols and the Names of the Creator, which can bring Terror and Fear unto you. Obey me then, by the power of these Holy Names, and by these *Mysterious Symbols* of the *Secret* of *Secrets*.

The which being said and done, thou shalt see them draw near and approach from all parts. But if they be hindered, detained, or occupied in some way, and so that they cannot come, or if they are unwilling to come, then, the Suffumigations and Censings being performed anew, and (the Disciples) having anew, by especial order, touched their Swords, and the Master having encouraged his Disciples, he shall reform the Circle with the Knife of Art, and, raising the said Knife towards the Sky, he shall as it were strike the air therewith. After this he shall lay his hand upon the Pentacles, and having bent his knees before the Most High, he shall repeat with humility the following Confession; the which his Disciples shall also do, and they shall recite it in a low and humble voice, so that they can scarcely be heard.*

* So as not to interfere with the direction of the Will-currents of the Master.

BOOK ONE.

CHAPTER IV.

The Confession to be Made by the Exorcist.

CONFESSION.

O Lord of Heaven and of Earth, before Thee do I confess my sins, and lament them, cast down and humbled in thy presence. For I have sinned before Thee by pride, avarice, and boundless desire of honours and riches; by idleness, gluttony, greed, debauchery, and drunkenness; because I have offended Thee by all kinds of sins of the flesh, adulteries, and pollu-tions, which I have committed myself, and consented that others should commit; by sacrilege, thefts, rapine, violation, and homicide; by the evil use I have made of my possessions, by my prodigality, by the sins which I have committed against Hope and Charity, by my evil advice, flatteries, bribes, and the ill distribution which I have made of the goods of which I have been possessed; by repulsing and maltreating the poor, in the distri-bution which I have made of the goods committed to my charge, by afflict- ing those over whom I have been set in authority, by not visiting the prison-ers, by depriving the dead of burial, by not receiving the poor, by neither feeding the hungry nor giving drink to the thirsty, by never keeping the Sabbath and the other feasts, by not living chastely and piously on those days, by the easy consent which I have given to those who incited me to evil deeds, by injuring instead of aiding those who demanded help from me, by refusing to give ear unto the cry of the poor, by not respecting the aged, by not keeping my word, by disobedience to my parents, by ingrati-tude towards those from whom I have received kindness, by indulgence in sensual pleasures, by irreverend behaviour in the Temple of God, by un-seemly gestures thereat, by entering therein without reverence, by vain and unprofitable discourse when there, by despising the sacred vessels of the temple, by turning the holy Ceremonies into ridicule, by touching and eating the sacred bread with impure lips and with profane hands, and by the neglect of my prayers and adorations.

I detest also the crimes which I have committed by evil thoughts, vain and impure meditations, false suspicions, and rash judgments; by the evil consent which I have readily given unto the advice of the wicked, by lust of impure and sensual pleasures; by my idle words, my lies, and my deceit; by my false vows in various ways; and by my continual slander and calumny.

I detest also the crimes which I have committed within; the treachery and discord which I have incited; my curiosity, greed, false speaking, vio-lence, malediction, murmurs, blasphemies, vain words, insults, dissimula-tions; my sins against God by the transgression of the ten commandments, by neglect of my duties and obligations, and by want of love towards God and towards my neighbour.

Furthermore I hate the sins which I have committed in all my senses, by sight, by hearing, by taste, by smell, and by touch, in every way that human weakness can offend the Creator; by my carnal thoughts, deeds, and meditations.

In which I humbly confess that I have sinned, and recognise myself as being in the sight of God the most criminal of all men.

I accuse myself before Thee, O God, and I adore Thee with all humility. O ye, Holy Angels, and ye, Children of God, in your presence I publish my sins, so that mine Enemy may have no advantage over me, and may not be able to reproach me at the last day; that he may not be able to say that I have concealed my sins, and that I be not then accused in the presence of the Lord; but, on the contrary, that on my account there may be joy in Heaven, as over the just who have confessed their sins in thy presence.

O Most Mighty and All Powerful Father, grant through Thine unbounded Mercy that I may both see and know all the Spirits which I invoke, so that by their means I may see my will and desire accomplished, by The Sovereign grandeur, and by Thine Ineffable and Eternal Glory, Thou Who art and Who wilt be for ever the Pure and Ineffable Father of All.

The Confession having been finished with great humility, and with the inward feeling of the heart, the Master will recite the following prayer:—

PRAYER.

O Lord All Powerful, Eternal God and Father of all Creatures, shed upon me the Divine Influence of Thy Mercy, for I am Thy Creature. I beseech Thee to defend me from mine Enemies, and to confirm in me true and steadfast faith.

O Lord, I commit my Body and my Soul unto Thee, seeing I put my trust in none beside Thee; it is on Thee alone that I rely; O Lord my God aid me; O Lord hear me in the day and hour wherein I shall invoke Thee. I pray Thee by Thy Mercy not to put me in oblivion, nor to remove me from Thee. O Lord be Thou my succor, Thou Who art the God of my salvation. O Lord make me a new heart according unto Thy loving Kindness. These, O Lord, are the gifts which I await from Thee, O my God and my Master, Thou Who livest and reignest unto the Ages of the Ages. Amen.

O Lord God the All Powerful One, Who hast formed unto Thyself great and Ineffable Wisdom, and Co-eternal with Thyself before the countless Ages; Thou Who in the Birth of Time hast created the Heavens, and the Earth, the Sea, and things that they contain; Thou who hast vivified all things by the Breath of Thy Mouth, I praise Thee, I bless Thee, I adore Thee, and I glorify Thee. Be Thou propitious unto me who am but a miserable sinner, and despise me not; save me and succor me, even me the work of Thine hands. I conjure and entreat Thee by Thy Holy Name to banish from my Spirit the darkness of Ignorance, and to enlighten me with the Fire of thy Wisdom; take away from me all evil desires, and let not my speech be as that of the foolish. O Thou, God the Living One, Whose Glory, Honour, and Kingdom shall extend unto the Ages of the Ages. Amen.

BOOK ONE.

CHAPTER V.

Prayers and Conjurations.

PRAYER.

O Lord God, Holy Father, Almighty and Merciful One, Who hast created all things, Who knowest all things and can do all things, from Whom nothing is hidden, to Whom nothing is impossible; Thou who knowest that we perform not these ceremonies to tempt Thy power, but that we may penetrate into the knowledge of hidden things; we pray Thee by Thy Sacred Mercy to cause and to permit, that we may arrive at this understanding of secret things, of whatever nature they may be by Thine aid, O Most Holy Adonai, Whose Kingdom and Power shall have no end unto the Ages of the Ages. Amen.

The Prayer being finished, let the Exorcist lay his hand upon the Pentacles, while one of the Disciples shall hold open before him the Book wherein are written the prayers and conjurations proper for conquering, subduing, and reproving the Spirits. Then the Master, turning towards each Quarter of the Earth, and raising his eyes to Heaven, shall say:

O Lord, be Thou unto me a strong tower of refuge, from the sight and assaults of the Evil Spirits.

After which let him turn again towards the Four Quarters of the Earth, and towards each let him utter the following words:

Behold the Symbols and Names of the Creator, which give unto ye forever Terror and Fear. Obey then, by the virtue of these Holy Names, and by these Mysteries of Mysteries.

After this he shall see the Spirits come from every side. But in case they are occupied in some other place, or that they cannot come, or that they are unwilling to come: then let him commence afresh to invoke them after the following manner, and let the Exorcist be assured that even were they bound with chains of iron, and with fire, they could not refrain from coming to accomplish his will.

THE CONJURATION.*

O ye Spirits, ye I conjure by the Power, Wisdom, and Virtue of the Spirit of God, by the uncreate Divine Knowledge, by the vast Mercy of

* There is an Invocation bearing the title of "The Qabalistical Invocation of Solomon," given by Eliphas Lévi, which differs in many points from the one given above, though resembling it in some particulars. Lévi's is more evidently constructed on the plan indicated in the "Siphra Dtzenioutha," c. III.; Annotation § 5, sub. § 8, 9; while the one above more follows that laid down, *ibid.* § 5, sub. § 3. I see no reason to suppose that Lévi's is unauthentic. It will be noted by the Qabalistical reader, that the above Conjuration rehearses the Divine Names attached to the Ten Sephiroth.

God, by the Strength of God, by the Greatness of God, by the Unity of God; and by the Holy Name of God EHEIEH, which is the root, trunk, source, and origin of all the other Divine Names, whence they all draw their life and their virtue, which Adam having invoked, he acquired the knowledge of all created things.

I conjure ye by the Indivisible Name IOD, which marketh and expresseth the Simplicity and the Unity of the Nature Divine, which Abel having invoked, he deserved* to escape from the hands of Cain his brother.

I conjure ye by the Name TETRAGRAMMATON ELOHIM, which expresseth and signifieth the Grandeur of so lofty a Majesty, that Noah having pronounced it, saved himself, and protected himself with his whole household from the Waters of the Deluge.

I conjure ye by the Name of God EL Strong and Wonderful, which denoteth the Mercy and Goodness of His Majesty Divine, which Abraham having invoked, he was found worthy to come forth from the Ur of the Chaldeans.

I conjure ye by the most powerful Name of ELOHIM GIBOR, which showeth forth the Strength of God, of a God All Powerful, Who punisheth the crimes of the wicked, Who seeketh out and chastiseth the iniquities of the fathers upon the children unto the third and fourth generation; which Isaac having invoked, he was found worthy to escape from the Sword of Abraham his father.

I conjure ye and I exorcise ye by the most holy Name of ELOAH VA-DAATH, which Jacob invoked when in great trouble, and was found worthy to bear the Name of Israel, which signifieth Vanquisher of God; and he was delivered from the fury of Esau his brother.

I conjure ye by the most potent Name of EL† ADONAI TZABAOTH, which is the God of Armies, ruling in the Heavens, which Joseph invoked and was found worthy to escape from the hands of his Brethren.

I conjure ye by the most potent Name of ELOHIM TZABAOTH, which expresseth piety, mercy, splendour, and knowledge of God, which Moses invoked, and he was found worthy to deliver the People Israel from Egypt, and from the servitude of Pharaoh.

I conjure ye by the most potent Name of SHADDAI, which signifieth doing good unto all; which Moses invoked, and having struck the Sea, it divided into two parts in the midst, on the right hand and on the left. I conjure ye by the most holy Name of EL‡ CHAI, which is that of the Living God, through the virtue of which alliance with us, and redemption for us have been made; which Moses invoked and all the waters returned to their prior state and enveloped the Egyptians, so that not one of them escaped to carry the news into the Land of Mizraim.

Lastly, I conjure ye all, ye rebellious Spirits, by the most holy Name

* In the French, "merita d'échapper."

† More usually the Name TETRAGRAMMATON TZABAOTH is attributed to the Seventh Sephira.

‡ Both this Name and "Shaddai" are attributed to the Ninth Sephira, and I have therefore put the two invocations in the same paragraph.

of God ADONAI MELEKH, which Joshua invoked, and stayed the course of the Sun in his presence, through the virtue of Methratton,* its principal Image; and by the troops of Angels who cease not to cry day and night, QADOSCH, SADOSCH, QADOSCH, ADONAI ELOHIM TZABAOTH (that is, Holy, Holy, Holy, Lord God of Hosts, Heaven and Earth are full of Thy Glory); and by the Ten Angels who preside over the Ten Sephiroth, by whom God communicateth and extendeth His influence over lower things, which are KETHER, CHOKMAH, BINAH, GEDULAH, GEBURAH, TIPHERETH, NETZACH, HOD, YESOD, AND MALKUTH.

I conjure ye anew, O Spirits, by all the Names of God, and by all His marvellous work; by the heavens; by the earth; by the sea; by the depth of the Abyss, and by that firmament which the very Spirit of God hath moved; by the sun and by the stars; by the waters and by the seas, and all which they contain; by the winds, the whirlwinds, and the tempests; by the virtue of all herbs, plants, and stones; by all which is in the heavens, upon the earth, and in all the Abysses of the Shades.

I conjure ye anew, and I powerfully urge ye, O Demons, in whatsoever part of the world ye may be, so that ye shall be unable to remain in air, fire, water, earth, or in any part of the universe, or in any pleasant place which may attract ye; but that ye come promptly to accomplish our desire, and all things that we demand from your obedience.

I conjure ye anew by the two Tables of the Law, by the five books of Moses, by the Seven Burning Lamps on the Candlestick of Gold before the face of the Throne of the Majesty of God, and by the Holy of Holies wherein the KOHEN HA-GADUL was alone permitted to enter, that is to say, the High-Priest.

I conjure ye by Him Who hath made the heavens and the earth, and who hath measured those heavens in the hollow of His hand, and enclosed the earth with three of His fingers, Who is seated upon the Kerubim and upon the Seraphim; and by the Kerubim, which is called the Kerub, which God constituted and placed to guard the Tree of Life, armed with a flaming sword, after that Man had been driven out of Paradise.

I conjure ye anew, Apostates from God, by Him Who alone hath performed great wonders; by the Heavenly Jerusalem; and by the Most Holy Name of God in Four Letters, and by Him Who enlighteneth all things and shineth upon all things by his Venerable and Ineffable Name, EHEIEH ASHER EHEIEH; that ye come immediately to execute our desire, whatever it may be.

I conjure ye, and I command ye absolutely, O Demons, in whatsoever part of the Universe ye may be, by the virtue of all these Holy Names;—ADONAI,† YAH, HOA, EL, ELOHA, ELOHINU, ELOHIM, EHEIEH, MARON,

* The Archangel, who is called also the Prince of Countenances.

† I have made these Names as correct as possible; as in all the original MSS. the Hebrew is much mutilated. These names are some of them ordinary titles of God; others Magical and Qabalistical names compounded from the initials of sentences, &c.; and others permutations of other names.

KAPHU, ESCH, INNON, AVEN, AGLA, HAZOR, EMETH, YAH, ARARITHA, YOVA, HA-KABIR, MESSIACH, IONAH, MAL-KA, EREL, KUZU, MATZ-PATZ, EL SHADDAI; and by all the Holy names of God which have been written with blood in the sign of an eternal alliance.

I conjure ye anew by these other names of God, Most Holy and unknown, by the virtue of which Names ye tremble every day;—BARUC,* BACURABON, PATACEL, ALCHEEGHEL, AQUACHAI, HOMORION, EHEIEH, ABBATON, CHEVON, CEBON, OYZROYMAS, CHAI, EHEIEH, ALBAMACHI, ORTAGU, NALE, ABELECH (or HELECH), YEZE (or SECHEZZE); that ye come quickly and without any delay into our presence from every quarter and every climate of the world wherein ye may be, to execute all that we shall command ye in the Great Name of God.

* I give these Names as they stand, they do not all appear to be Hebrew; some of them suggest the style of the barbarous names in the Græco-Egyptian Magical Papyri.

BOOK ONE.

CHAPTER VI.

Stronger and More Potent Conjuration.

If they then immediately appear, it is well; if not, let the Master uncover the consecrated *Pentacles* which he should have made to constrain and command the Spirits, and which he should wear fastened round his neck, holding the Medals (or Pentacles) in his left hand, and the consecrated Knife in his right; and encouraging his Companions, he shall say with a loud voice:—

ADDRESS.

Here be the Symbols of Secret things, the standards, the ensigns, and the banners, of God the Conqueror; and the arms of the Almighty One, to compel the *Aerial Potencies.* I command ye absolutely by their power and virtue that ye come near unto us, into our presence, from whatsoever part of the world ye may be in, and that ye delay not to obey us in all things wherein we shall command ye by the virtue of God the Mighty One. Come ye promptly, and delay not to appear, and answer us with humility.

If they appear at this time, show them the Pentacles, and receive them with kindness, gentleness, and courtesy; reason and speak with them, question them, and ask from them all things which thou hast proposed to demand.

But if, on the contrary, they do not yet make their appearance, holding the consecrated Knife in the right hand, and the *Pentacles* being uncovered by the removal of their consecrated covering, strike and beat the air with the Knife as if wishing to commence a combat, comfort and exhort thy Companions, and then in a loud and stern voice repeat the following Conjuration:—

CONJURATION.*

Here again I conjure ye and most urgently command ye; I force, constrain, and exhort ye to the utmost, by the most mighty and powerful Name of God El, strong and wonderful, and by God the Just and Upright, I exorcise ye and command ye that ye in no way delay, but that ye come immediately and upon the instant hither before us, without noise, deformity, or hideousness, but with all manner of gentleness and mildness.

I exorcise ye anew, and powerfully conjure ye, commanding ye with strength and violence by Him Who spake and it was done; and by all these names: El, Shaddai, Elohim, Elohi, Tzabaoth, Elim, Asher Eheieh, Yah, Tetragrammaton, Shaddai, which signify God the High and

* This Conjuration is almost identical with one given in the "Lemegeton," or Lesser Key, a different work, also attributed to Solomon.

Almighty, the God of Israel, through Whom undertaking all our operations we shall prosper in all the works of our hands, seeing that the Lord is now, always, and for ever with us, in our heart and in our lips; and by His Holy Names, and by the virtue of the Sovereign God, we shall accomplish all our work.

Come ye at once without any hideousness or deformity before us, come ye without monstrous appearance, in a gracious form or figure. Come ye, for we exorcise ye with the utmost vehemence by the Name of IAH and ON, which Adam spake and heard; by the Name EL, which Noah heard, and saved himself with all his family from the Deluge; by the Name IOD, which Noah heard, and knew God the Almighty One; by the Name AGLA, which Jacob heard, and saw the Ladder which touched Heaven, and the Angels who ascended and descended upon it, whence he called that place the House of God and the Gate of Heaven; and by the Name ELOHIM, and in the Name ELOHIM, which Moses named, invoked, and heard in Horeb the Mount of God, and he was found worthy to hear Him speak from the Burning Bush; and by the Name AIN SOPH, which Aaron heard, and was at once made eloquent, wise, and learned; and by the Name TZABAOTH, which Moses named and invoked, and all the ponds and rivers were covered with blood throughout the land of Egypt;* and by the name IOD, which Moses named and invoked, and striking upon the dust of the earth both men and beasts were struck with disease;† and by the Name, and in the Name PRIMEUMATON, which Moses named and invoked, and there fell a great and severe hail throughout all the land of Egypt, destroying the vines, the trees, and the woods which were in that country; and by the Name IAPHAR, which Moses heard and invoked, and immediately a great pestilence began to appear through all the land of Egypt, striking and slaying the asses, the oxen, and the sheep of the Egyptians, so that they all died; and by the Name ABADDON which Moses invoked and sprinkled the dust towards heaven, and immediately there fell so great rain upon the men, cattle, and flocks, that they all died throughout the land of Egypt; and by the Name ELION which Moses invoked, and there fell so great hail as had never been seen from the beginning of the world unto that time, so that all men, and herds, and everything that was in the fields perished and died throughout all the land of Egypt. And by the Name EDONAL, which Moses having invoked, there came so great a quantity of locusts which appeared in the land of Egypt, that they devoured and swallowed up all that the hail had spared; and by the Name of PATHEON,‡ which having invoked, there arose so thick, so awful, and so terrible darkness throughout the land of Egypt, during the space of three days and three nights, that almost all who were left alive died; and

* Some MSS. add. "et furent purifiés."

† Some MSS. substitute, "les hommes furent reduits en cendre, comme aussi les bœufs, betail, et troupeaux des Egyptiens."

‡ This is often written PATHTUMON in similar Conjurations, but the MSS. before me agree in giving this form.

by the Name YESOD and in the Name YESOD, which Moses invoked, and at midnight all the first-born, both of men and of animals, died; and by the Name of YESHIMON, which Moses named and invoked, and the Red Sea divided itself and separated in two; and by the name HESION, which Moses invoked, and all the army of Pharaoh was drowned in the waters; and by the Name ANABONA, which Moses having heard upon Mount Sinai, he was found worthy to receive and obtain the tables of stone written with the finger of God the Creator; and by the Name ERYGION, which Joshua having invoked when he fought against the Moabites, he defeated them and gained the victory; and by the Name HOA, and in the Name HOA, which David invoked, and he was delivered from the hand of Goliath; and by the name YOD, which Solomon having named and invoked, he was found worthy to ask for and obtain in sleep the Ineffable Wisdom of God; and by the Name YIAI, which Solomon having named and invoked, he was found worthy to have power over all the Demons, Potencies, Powers, and Virtues of the Air.

By these, then, and by all the other Names of God Almighty, Holy, Living, and True, we powerfully command ye, ye who by your own sin have been cast down from the Empyreal Heaven, and from before His Throne; by Him who hath cast ye down unto the most profound of the Abysses of Hell, we command ye boldly and resolutely; and by that terrible Day of the Sovereign Judgment of God, on which all the dry bones in the earth will arise to hear and listen unto the Word of God with their body, and will present themselves before the face of God Almighty; and by that Last Fire which shall consume all things; by the (Crystal) Sea which is known unto us, which is before the Face of God; by the indicible and ineffable virtue, force, and power of the Creator Himself, by His Almighty power, and by the Light and Flame which emanate from His Countenance, and which are before His Face; by the Angelical Powers which are in the Heavens, and by the most great Wisdom of Almighty God; by the Seal of David, by the Ring and Seal of Solomon, which was revealed unto him by the Most High and Sovereign Creator; and by the Nine Medals or Pentacles, which we have among our Symbols, which proceed and come from Heaven, and are among the Mysteries of Mysteries or Secrets of Secrets, which you can also behold in my hand, consecrated and exorcised with the due and requisite Ceremonies. By these, then, and by all the Secrets which the Almighty encloseth in the Treasures of the Sovereign and Highest Wisdom, by His Hand, and by His marvellous power; I conjure, force, and exorcise ye that ye come without delay to perform in our presence that which we shall command ye.

I conjure ye anew by that most Holy Name which the whole Universe fears, respects, and reveres, which is written by these letters and characters, IOD, HE, VAU, HE; and by the last and terrible judgment; by the Seat of BALDACHIA;* and by this Holy Name, YIAI, which Moses invoked, and

* Sometimes, but as I think erroneously, written Bas-dathea. I imagine the word to mean "Lord of Life."

there followed that great Judgment of God, when Dathan and Abiram were swallowed up in the centre of the earth. Otherwise, if ye contravene and resist us by your disobedience unto the virtue and power of this Name YIAI, we curse ye even unto the Depth of the Great Abyss, into the which we shall cast, hurl, and bind ye, if ye show yourselves rebellious against the Secret of Secrets, and against the Mystery of Mysteries. AMEN AMEN. FIAT, FIAT.

This Conjuration thou shalt say and perform, turning thyself unto the East, and if they appear not, thou shalt repeat it unto the Spirits, turning unto the South, the West, and the North, in succession, when thou wilt have repeated it four times. And if they appear not even then, thou shalt make the Sign of TAU* upon the foreheads of thy companions, and thou shalt say:—

CONJURATION.

Behold anew the Symbol and the Name of a Sovereign and Conquering God, through which all the Universe fears, trembles, and shudders, and through the most mysterious words of the Secret Mysteries and by their Virtue, Strength, and Power.

I conjure ye anew, I constrain and command ye with the utmost vehemence and power, by that most potent and powerful Name of God, EL, strong and wonderful, by Him who spake and it was done; and by the Name IAH, which Moses heard, and spoke with God; and by the Name AGLA, which Joseph invoked, and was delivered out of the hands of his brethren; and by the Name VAU, which Abraham heard, and knew God the Almighty One; and by the Name of Four Letters, TETRAGRAMMATON, which Joshua named and invoked, and he was rendered worthy and found deserving to lead the Army of Israel into the Promised Land; and by the Name ANABONA, by which God formed Man and the whole Universe; and by the Name ARPHETON,† and in the Name ARPHETON, by which the Angels who are destined to that end will summon the Universe, in visible body and form, and will assemble (all people) together by the sound of the Trumpet at that terrible and awful Day of Judgment, when the memory of the wicked and ungodly shall perish; and by the Name ADONAI, by which God will judge all human flesh, at Whose voice all men, both good and evil, will rise again, and all men and Angels will assemble in the air before the Lord, Who will judge and condemn the wicked; and by the Name ONEIPHETON,‡ by which God will summon the dead, and raise them up again unto life; and by the Name ELOHIM, and in the Name ELOHIM, by which God will disturb and excite tempests throughout all the seas, so that they will cast out the fish therefrom, and in one day the third part of men about the sea and the rivers shall die; and by the Name

* Or the Cross.

† Also written *Hipeton;* and I believe sometimes replaced by *Anapheneton*, or *Anaphaxeton*.

‡ This word is given variously in the MSS. as *Oneypheon*, *Onayepheton*, and *Donecepheron*, &c.

ELOHI,* and in the Name ELOHI, by which God will dry up the sea and the rivers, so that men can go on foot through their channels; and by the Name ON, and in the Name ON, by which God shall restore and replace the sea, the rivers, the streams, and the brooks, in their previous state; and by the Name MESSIACH,† and in the Name MESSIACH, by which God will make all animals combat together, so that they shall die in a single day; and by the Name ARIEL, by which God shall destroy in a single day all buildings, so that there shall not be left one stone upon another; and by the Name IAHT,‡ by which God will cast one stone upon another, so that all people and nations will fly from the sea-shore, and will say unto them cover us and hide us; and by the Name EMANUEL, by which God will perform wonders, and the winged creatures and birds of the air shall contend with one another; and by the Name ANAEL,§ and in the Name ANAEL, by which God will cast down the mountains and fill up the valleys, so that the surface of the earth shall be level in all parts; and by the Name ZEDEREZA,‖ and in the Name ZEDEREZA, by which God will cause the Sun and Moon to be darkened, and the Stars of heaven to fall; and by the Name SEPHERIEL,¶ by which God will come to Universal Judgment, like a Prince newly crowned entering in triumph into his capital city, girded with a zone of gold, and preceded by Angels, and at His aspect all climes and parts of the Universe shall be troubled and astonished, and a fire shall go forth before Him, and flames and storm shall surround Him; and by the Name TAU,** by which God brought the Deluge, and the waters prevailed above the mountains, and fifteen cubits above their summits; and by the Name RUACHIAH,†† by which God having purged the Ages, He will make His Holy spirit to descend upon the Universe, and will cast ye, ye rebellious Spirits, and unclean beings, into the Depths of the Lake of the Abyss, in misery, filth, and mire, and will place ye in impure and foul dungeons bound with eternal chains of fire.

By these Names then, and by all the other Holy Names of God before Whom no man can stand and live, and which Names the armies of the Demons fear, tremble at, and shudder; we conjure ye, we potently exorcise and command ye, conjuring ye in addition by the terrible and tremendous PATHS‡‡ of GOD and by His Holy habitation wherein He reigneth and commandeth unto the eternal Ages. Amen.

* Or *Elia*.

† What is said here refers symbolically to the rooting out of the Evil Spirits, and Shells, from the Universe by King Messiach, which is spoken of in the Qabalah. The Qabalah sometimes expresses the Evil Spirits by the words animals, or beasts, and creeping things.

‡ The oldest MSS. gives the above form, in the others it is changed into *Iaphat, Taphat,* and even *Japhet*. It is probably a corruption of *Achad* Unity.

§ This is also the name of the Angel of Venus.

‖ So written in the oldest MS., the others give it as *Zedeesia, Zedeezia,* and *Zedezias*.

¶ Meaning "emanating from God." It is corrupted into *Sephosiel*, &c., in the MSS.

** *Iaha*, in 10862 Add. MSS.

†† Meaning Spirit of Iah.

‡‡ That is, the hidden and occult grades and links of emanation in the Sephiroth. The later MSS. have put, by mistake, *voix* for *voies*, the oldest Latin MS. gives Semitis.

By the virtue of all these aforesaid, we command ye that ye remain not in any place wherein ye are, but to come hither promptly without delay to do that which we shall enjoin ye. But if ye be still contumacious, we, by the Authority of a Sovereign and Potent God, deprive ye of all quality, condition, degree, and place which ye now enjoy, and precipitate ye into and relegate ye unto the Kingdom of Fire and of Sulphur, to be there eternally tormented. Come ye then from all parts of the earth, wheresoever ye may be, and behold the Symbols and Names of that Triumphant Sovereign Whom all creatures obey, otherwise we shall bind ye and conduct ye in spite of yourselves, into our presence bound with chains of fire, because those effects which proceed and issue from our Science and operation, are ardent with a fire which shall consume and burn ye eternally, for by these the whole Universe trembleth, the earth is moved, the stones thereof rush together, all creatures obey, and the rebellious Spirits are tormented by the power of the *Sovereign Creator.*

Then it is certain that they will come, even if they be bound with chains of fire, unless prevented by affairs of the very greatest importance, but in this latter case they will send ambassadors and messengers by whom thou shalt easily and surely learn what occupies the Spirits and what they are about. But if they appear not yet in answer to the above Conjuration, and are still disobedient, then let the Master of the Art or Exorciser arise and exhort his Companions to be of good cheer and not to despair of the ultimate success of the operation; let him strike the air with the *Consecrated Knife* towards the Four Quarters of the Universe; and then let him Kneel in the midst of the Circle, and the Companions also in their several places, and let them say consecutively with him in a low voice, turning in the direction of the East, the following

ADDRESS TO THE ANGELS.

I conjure and pray ye, O ye Angels of God, and ye Celestial Spirits, to come unto mine aid; come and behold the Signs of Heaven, and be my witness before the Sovereign Lord, of the disobedience of these evil and fallen Spirits who were at one time your companions.

This being done, let the Master arise, and constrain and force them by a stronger conjuration, in manner following.

BOOK ONE.

CHAPTER VII.

An Extremely Powerful Conjuration.

BEHOLD us again prepared to conjure ye by the Names and Symbols of God, wherewith we are fortified, and by the virtue of the Highest One. We command ye and potently ordain ye by the most strong and powerful Names of God, Who is worthy of all praise, admiration, honor, glory, veneration, and fear, that ye delay not longer, but that ye appear before us without any tumult or disturbance, but, on the contrary, with great respect and courtesy, in a beautiful and human form.

If they then appear, let them see the Pentacles, and say:

Obey ye, Obey ye, behold the Symbols and Names of the Creator; be ye gentle and peaceable, and obey in all things that we shall command ye.

They will then immediately talk with thee, as a friend speaketh unto a friend. Ask of them all that thou desirest, with constancy, firmness, and assurance, and they will obey thee.

But if they appear not yet, let not the Master on that account lose his courage, for there is nothing in the world stronger and of greater force to overawe the Spirits than constancy. Let him, however, re-examine and reform the Circle, and let him take up a little dust of the earth, which he shall cast towards the Four Quarters of the Universe; and having placed his Knife upon the ground, let him say on his knees, turning towards the direction of the North:

In the Name of ADONAI ELOHIM TZABAOTH SHADDAI, Lord God of Armies Almighty, may we successfully perform the works of our hands. and may the Lord be present with us in our heart and in our lips.

These words having been said kneeling upon the earth, let the Master shortly after arise and open his arms wide as if wishing to embrace the air, and say:

CONJURATION.

By the Holy Names of God written in this Book, and by the other Holy and Ineffable Names which are written in the Book of Life, we conjure ye to come unto us promptly and without any delay, wherefore tarry not, but appear in a beautiful and agreeable form the figure, by these Holy Names: ADONAI, TZABAOTH, EL, ELOHI, ELOHIM, SHADDAI; and by EHEIEH, YOD HE VAU HE which is the Great Name of God TETRAGRAMMATION written with Four Letters, ANAPHODITION, and Ineffable; by the God of those Virtues and Potencies, Who dwelleth in the Heavens, Who rideth upon the Kerubim, Who moveth upon the Wings of the Wind, He Whose Power is in Heaven and in Earth, Who spake and it was done, Who commanded and the whole Universe was created; and by the Holy Names and in the Holy Names, IAH, IAH, IAH, ADONAI TZABAOTH; and by all the Names of God, the Living, and the True, I reiterate the Conjuration, and I conjure ye afresh ye Evil and rebellious Spirits, abiding in the Abysses of Darkness.

I conjure, I address, and I exorcise ye, that ye may approach unto and come before the Throne of God, the Living and the True, and before the Tribunal of the Judgment of His Majesty, and before the Holy Angels of God to hear the sentence of your condemnation.

Come ye then by the Name and in the Name of SHADDA. which is that of God Almighty, strong, powerful, admirable, exalted, pure, clean, glorified, virtuous, great, just, terrible, and holy; and by the Name and in the Name of EL, IAH, IAH, IAH, Who hath formed and created the world by the Breath of His Mouth, Who supporteth it by His Power, Who ruleth and governeth it by His Wisdom, and Who hath cast ye for your pride into the *Land of Darkness* and into the *Shadow of Death.*

Therefore, by the Name of the Living God, Who hath formed the heavens above, and hath laid the foundations of the earth beneath, we command ye that, immediately and without any delay, ye come unto us from all places, valleys, mountains, hills, field, seas, rivers, fountains, ponds, brooks, caverns, grottos, cities, towns, villages, markets, fairs, habitations, baths, courtyards, gardens, vineyards, plantations, reservoirs, cisterns, and from every corner of the terrestrial earth where ye may happen to be in your assemblies, so that ye may execute and accomplish our demands with all mildness and courtesy; by that Ineffable Name which Moses heard and invoked, which he received from God from the midst of the Burning Bush, we conjure ye to obey our commands, and to come unto us promptly with all gentleness of manner.

Again we command ye with vehemence, and we exorcise ye with constancy, that ye and all your comrades come unto us in an agreeable and gracious manner like the breeze, to accomplish successively our various commands and desires. Come ye, then, by the virtue of these Names by the which we exorcise ye; ANAI, ÆCHHAD, TRANSIN, EMETH, CHAIA, IONA, PROFA, TITACHE, BEN ANI, BRIAH, THEIT; all which names are written in Heaven in the characters of Malachim,* that is to say, the tongue of the Angels.

We then, by the just judgment of God, by the Ineffiable and Admirable Virtue of God, just, living, and true, we call ye with power, we force and exorcise ye by and in the admirable Name which was written on the Tables of Stone which God gave upon Mount Sinai; and by and in the wonderful Name which Aaron the High Priest bare written upon his breast, by which also God created the World, the which name is AXINETON; and by the Living God Who is One throughout the Ages, whose dwelling is in the Ineffable Light, Whose Name is Wisdom, and Whose Spirit is Life, before Whom goeth forth Fire and Flame, Who hath from that Fire formed the firmament, the Stars and the Sun; and Who with that Fire will burn ye all for ever, as also all who shall contravene the Words of His Will.

Come ye, then, without delay, without noise, and without rage, before us, without any deformity or hideousness, to execute all our will; come ye

* The Mystic Alphabet known as the "Writing of Malachim" is formed from the positions of the Stars in the heavens, by drawing imaginary lines from one star to another so as to obtain the shapes of the characters of this Alphabet.

from all places wherein ye are, from all mountains, valleys, streams, rivers, brooks, ponds, places, baths, synagogues; for God, strong and powerful, will chase ye and constrain ye, being glorious over all things; He will compel ye, both ye and the Prince of Darkness. Come ye, come ye, Angels of Darkness; come hither before this Circle without fear, terror, or deformity, to execute our commands, and be ye ready both to achieve and to complete all that we shall command ye.

Come ye, then, by the Crown of the Chief of your Emperors, and by the Sceptres of your power, and of SID, the Great Demon, your Master; by the Names and in the Names of the Holy Angels who have been created to be above you, long before the constitution of the world; and by the Names of the two Princes of the Universe, whose Names are, IONIEL and SEFONIEL; by the rod of Moses, by the staff of Jacob; by the ring and seal of David, wherein are written the Names of Sovereign God; and by the Names of the Angels by which SOLOMON has linked and bound ye; and by the sacred bonds by which ANAEL hath environed and hath conquered the Spirit: and by the Name of the Angel who ruleth potently over the rest, and by the praise of all creatures who cry incessantly unto God, Who spake, and immediately all things, even the Ages, were made and formed; and by the Name HA-QADOSCH BERAKHA, which signifies the Holy and Blessed One; and by the Ten Choirs of the Holy Angels, CHAIOTH HA-QADESH, AUPHANIM, ARALIM, CHASHMALIM, SERAPHIM, MALACHIM, ELOHIM, BENI ELOHIM, KERUBIM, and ISHIM; and by, and in the Sacred name of Twelve Letters of which each Letter is the Name of an Angel, and the letters of the Name are ALEPH*, BETH, BETH, NUN, VAU, RESH, VAU, CHETH, HE, QOPH, DALETH, SHIN.

By these Names therefore, and by all the other Holy Names, we conjure ye and we exorcise ye; by the Angel ZECHIEL; by the Angel DUCHIEL; by the Angel DONACHIEL; and by the Great Angel METATRON, Who is the Prince of the Angels, and introduceth the Souls before the Face of God; and by the Angel SANGARIEL, by whom the portals of Heaven are guarded; and by the Angel KERUB, who was made the Guardian of the Terrestrial Paradise, with a Sword of Flame, after the expulsion of Adam our forefather; and by the Angel MICHAEL by whom ye were hurled down from the Height of the THRONE into the Depth of the Lake and of the Abyss, the same Name meaning, "Who is like God upon Earth;" and by the Angel ANIEL; and by the Angel OPHIEL; and by the Angel BEDALIEL; wherefore, by these and by all the other Holy Names of the Angels, we powerfully conjure and exorcise ye, that ye come from all parts of the world immediately, and without any delay, to perform our will and demands, obeying us quickly and courteously, and that ye come by the Name and in the Name of ALEPH, DALETH, NUN, IOD, for we

* Which Letters I have, with much care, corrected, for in the MSS. the letters are jumbled together in hopeless confusion, *Seym* is written for *Shin*, *Res* for *Beth*, &c. The Name is *Ab, Ben, Ve-Ruach, Ha-Qadesch,* Father, Son, and Holy Spirit. There are two other Names of Twelve Letters frequently employed, HQDVSH BRVK HVA, Holy and Blessed be He; and ADNI HMLK NAMN, The Lord, the faithful King; besides other forms.

exorcise ye anew by the application of these Letters, by whose power burning fire is quenched, and the whole Universe trembleth.

We constrain ye yet again by the Seal of the Sun which is the Word of God; and by the Seal of the Moon and of the Stars we bind ye; and by the other Animals and Creatures which are in Heaven, by whose wings Heaven cleanseth itself, we force and attract ye imperiously to execute our will without failure. And we conjure, oblige, and terribly exorcise ye, that ye draw near unto us without delay and without fear, as far as is possible unto ye, here before this Circle, as supplicants gently and with discretion, to accomplish our will in all and through all. If ye come promptly and voluntarily, ye shall inhale our perfumes, and our suffumigations of pleasant odour, which will be both agreeable and delightful unto ye. Furthermore ye will see the Symbol of your Creator, and the Names of his Holy Angels, and we shall afterwards dismiss ye, and send ye hence with thanks. But if, on the contrary, ye come not quickly, and ye show yourselves self-opinionated, rebellious, and contumacious, we shall conjure ye again, and exorcise ye ceaselessly, and will repeat all the aforesaid words and Holy Names of God and of the Holy Angels; by the which Names we shall harass you, and if that be not sufficient we will add thereunto yet greater and more powerful ones, and we will thereunto again add other Names which ye have not yet heard from us, which are those of an Almighty God, and which will make ye tremble and quake with fear, both ye and your princes; by the which Names we conjure both you and them also, and we shall not desist from our work until the accomplishment of our will. But if perchance ye yet shall harden yourselves, and show yourselves self-opinionated, disobedient, rebellious, refractory, and contumacious, and if ye yet resist our powerful conjurations, we shall pronounce against you this warrant of arrest in the Name of God Almighty, and this definite sentence that ye shall fall into dangerous disease and leprosy, and that in sign of the Divine Vengeance ye shall all perish by a terrifying and horrible death, and that a fire shall consume and devour you on every side, and utterly crush you; and that by the Power of God, a flame shall go forth from His Mouth which shall burn ye up and reduce ye unto nothing in Hell. Wherefore delay ye not to come, for we shall not cease from these powerful conjurations until ye shall be obliged to appear against your will.

Thus then, therefore, we anew conjure and exorcise ye by and in the Holy Name of ON, which is interpreted and called God; by the Name and in the Name of EHEIEH, which is the true Name of God, "I am He Who is;" by and in the Ineffable Name of Four Letters YOD HE VAU HE, the Knowledge and understanding of which is hidden even from the Angels; by the Name and in the Name of EL, which signifieth and denoteth the powerful and consuming fire which issueth from His Countenance, and which shall be your ruin and destruction; and by the Light of the Angels which is kindled and taken ineffably from that flame of Divine ardour.

By these then, and by other most Holy Names which we pronounce against you from the bottom of our hearts, do we force and constrain ye, if ye be yet rebellious and disobedient. We conjure ye powerfully and strongly exorcise ye, that ye come unto us with joy and quickness, without fraud or deceit, in truth and not in error.

Come ye then, come ye, behold the Signs and the Names of your Creator, behold the *Holy Pentacles* by the virtue of which the Earth is moved, the trees thereof and the Abysses tremble. Come ye; come ye; come ye.

These things being thus done and performed, ye shall see the Spirits come from all sides in great haste with their Princes and Superiors; the Spirits of the First Order, like Soldiers, armed with spears, shields, and corslets; those of the Second Order like Barons, Princes, Dukes, Captains, and Generals of Armies. For the Third and last Order their King will appear, before whom go many players on instruments of music, accompanied by beautiful and melodious voices which sing in chorus.

Then the Exorcist, or Master of the Art, at the arrival of the King, whom he shall see crowned with a *Diadem,* should uncover the *Holy Pentacles* and Medals which he weareth upon his breast covered with a cloth of silk or of fine twined linen, and show them unto him, saying:—

Behold the Signs and Holy Names by and before whose power every knee should bow, of all that is in Heaven, upon Earth, or in Hell. Humble ye yourselves, therefore, under the Mighty hand of God.

Then will the King bow the knee before thee, and will say, "What dost thou wish, and wherefore hast thou caused us to come hither from the Infernal Abodes?"

Then shall the Exorcist, or Master of Magical Art, with an assured air and a grave and imperious voice, order and command him to be tranquil, to keep the rest of his attendants peaceable, and to impose silence upon them.

Let him, also, renew his fumigations, and offer large quantities of Incense, which he should at once place upon the fire, in order to appease the Spirits as he hath promised them. He should then cover the Pentacles, and he will see wonderful things, which it is impossible to relate, touching worldly matters and all sciences.

This being finished, let the Master uncover the Pentacles, and demand all that he shall wish from the King of the Spirits, and if there are one or two Spirits only, it will be the same; and having obtained all his desire, he shall thus license them to depart:—

THE LICENSE TO DEPART.

In the Name of ADONAI, the Eternal and Everlasting One, let each of you return unto his place; be there peace between us and you, and be ye ready to come when ye are called.

After this he should recite the first chapter of Genesis, "*Berashith Bara Elohim,* In the beginning, &c."

This being done, let them all in order quit the Circle, one after the other, the Master first. Furthermore let them bathe their faces with the exorcised water, as will be hereafter told, and then let them take their ordinary raiment and go about their business.

Take notice and observe carefully that this last conjuration is of so great importance and efficacy, that even if the Spirits were bound with chains of iron and fire, or shut up in some strong place, or retained by an oath, they could not even then delay to come. But supposing that they were being conjured in some other place or part of the Universe by some other Exorcist or Master of the Art, by the same conjuration; the Master should add to his conjuration that they should at least send him some Messengers, or some individual to declare unto him where they are, how employed, and the reason why they cannot come and obey him.

But if (which is almost impossible) they be even yet self-opinionated and disobedient, and unwilling to obey; in this case their names should be written on virgin paper, which he should soil and fill with mud, dust, or clay. Then he shall kindle a fire with dry rue, upon which he shall put powdered assafœtida, and other things of evil odour; after which let him put the aforesaid names, written on parchment* or *Virgin Parchment Paper,* upon the fire, saying:—

THE CONJURATION OF THE FIRE.

I conjure thee, O Creature of Fire, by Him who removeth the Earth, and maketh it tremble, that thou burn and torment these Spirits, so that they may feel it intensely, and that they may be burned eternally by thee.

This being said, thou shalt cast the aforesaid paper into the fire, saying:—

THE CURSE.

Be ye accursed, damned, and eternally reproved; and be ye tormented with perpetual pain, so that we may find no repose by night nor by day, nor for a single moment of time, if ye obey not immediately the command of Him Who maketh the Universe to tremble; by these Names, and in virtue of these Names, the which being named and invoked all creatures obey and tremble with fear and terror, these Names which can turn aside lightning and thunder; and which will utterly make you to perish, destroy, and banish you. These Names then are Aleph, Beth, Gimel, Daleth, He, Vau, Zayin, Cheth, Teth, Yod, Kaph, Lamed, Mem, Nun, Samekh, Ayin, Pe, Tzaddi, Qoph, Resh, Shin, Tau.†

By these secret Names, therefore, and by these signs which are full of Mysteries, we curse ye, and in virtue of the power of the Three Principles, Aleph,‡ Mem, Shin, we deprive ye of all office and dignity which ye may have enjoyed up till now; and by their virtue and power we relegate you unto a lake of sulphur and of flame, and unto the deepest depths of the Abyss, that ye may burn therein eternally for ever.

* Genuine Virgin Parchment is made from the skin of young Lambs and can be obtained from Messrs. de Laurence, Scott & Co.

† Which are the Names of the Letters of the Hebrew Alphabet, to each of which a special mystic meaning and power is attached, besides its ordinary application.

‡ The Literal Symbols of Air, Water, and Fire; which are called by the Sepher Yetzirah the Three Mother Letters.

Then will they assuredly come without any delay, and in great haste, crying: "O Our Lord and Prince, deliver us out of this suffering."

All this time thou shouldest have near thee ready an exorcised pen, paper, and ink, as will be described hereinafter. Write their Names afresh, and kindle fresh fire, whereon thou shalt put gum benjamin, olybdanum, and storax to make therewith a fumigation; with these odours thou shalt afresh, perfume the aforesaid paper with the Names; but thou shouldest have these names ready prepared beforehand. Then show them the Holy Pentacles, and ask of them what thou wilt, and thou shalt obtain it; and having gained thy purpose, send away the Spirits, saying:

THE LICENSE TO DEPART.

By the virtue of these *Pentacles,* and because ye have been obedient, and have obeyed the commandments of the Creator, feel and inhale this grateful odour, and afterwards depart ye unto your abodes and retreats; be there peace between us and you; be ye ever ready to come when ye shall be cited and called; and may the blessing of God, as far as ye are capable of receiving it, be upon you, provided ye be obedient and prompt to come unto us without solemn rites and observances on our part.

Thou shouldest further make a Book of Virgin Parchment* Paper, and therein write the foregoing conjurations, and constrain the Demons to swear upon the same book that they will come whenever they be called, and present themselves before thee, whenever thou shalt wish to consult them. Afterwards thou canst cover this Book with sacred Sigils on a plate of silver, and therein write or engrave the *Holy Pentacles.* Thou mayest open this Book either on Sundays or on Thursdays, rather at night than by day, and the Spirits will come.

Regarding the expression *"night,"* understand the night following, and not the night preceding the aforesaid days. And remember that by day (the Demons) are ashamed, for they are Animals of Darkness.

* This Book can be made from Genuine Virgin Parchment Paper which may be obtained from Messrs. de Laurence, Scott & Co. This Book may consist of sixteen pages and can be made, by stitching with black Silk thread, one sheet of Genuine Virgin Parchment Paper, which comes in eight pieces. The stitching you may do yourself. See Order No. 292, in Messrs. de Laurence, Scott & Co.'s Catalogue.

It should be understood, by the *Disciple* who readeth here, that there are many kinds of so-called Parchment Paper sold, but there is in existence only one kind of Parchment Paper, and this is the *Genuine Virgin Parchment.* The very same, being made from the skin of dead born lambs, and, is always used for making *Talismans, Charms* and *Pentacles.* The ancient Astrologers, and the old Masters of *Talismanic Magic* never used anything otherwise than *Genuine Virgin Parchment,* as it is known to be the only material that conforms to the requirements of *Occultism* and *Talismanic Magic.*

Genuine Virgin Parchment, made from the skin of dead born lambs, is very costly, rare, and difficult to obtain. It must first be polished with pumice stone at great labor and expense before its surface is fit to be engraved upon or before any tracings can be made thereon. Many foolishly hesitate to pay the price asked for a sheet of *Genuine Virgin Parchment* greatly preferring to pay less for worthless material; but gold is gold; diamonds are diamonds; and *Virgin Parchment is Virgin Parchment.* As gold is always worth its equivalent in money, and diamonds are always worth so much a *Karat,* so *Genuine Virgin Parchment Paper* is always worth so much a sheet.

Messrs. de Laurence, Scott & Co. are the only firm, as far as the writer knows, that is able to furnish the pure, unspotted, *Genuine Virgin Parchment Paper* made from the skin of dead born lambs. The cost for a sheet is not high considering its great value and the secret purposes for which it can be used. Whether you care to pay the price asked or not is entirely an affair of your own.

BOOK ONE.

CHAPTER VIII.

Concerning Pentacles, and the Manner of Constructing Them.

As we have already made mention of the *Pentacles,* it is necessary that thou shouldest understand that the whole Science and understanding of our "*Key*" dependeth upon the operation, Knowledge, and use of *Pentacles.*

He then who shall wish to perform any operation by the means of the *Medals,* or *Pentacles,* and therein to render himself expert, must observe what hath been hereinbefore ordained. Let him then, *O my Son Roboam,* know and understand that in the aforesaid *Pentacles* he shall find those Ineffable and Most Holy Names which were written by the finger of God in the *Tablets* of *Moses;* and which I, Solomon, have received through the Ministry of an Angel by Divine Revelation. These then have I collected together, arranged, consecrated, and kept, for the benefit of the human race, and the preservation of *Body* and of *Soul.*

The *Pentacles* should then be made in the days and hours of Mercury, when the Moon is in an *aërial** or terrestrial sign; she should also be in her increase, and in equal number of days with the Sun.

It is necessary to have a Chamber or Cabinet specially set apart and newly cleaned, wherein thou canst remain without interruption, the which having entered with thy Companions, thou shalt incense and perfume it with the odours and perfumes of the Art. The sky should be clear and serene. It is necessary that thou shouldest have one or more pieces of virgin paper prepared and arranged ready, as we shall tell you more fully later on, in its place.

Thou shalt commence the writing or construction of the *Pentacles* in the hour aforesaid. Among other things, thou shalt chiefly use these colours: Gold, Cinnabar or Vermilion Red, and celestial or brilliant Azure Blue. Furthermore, thou shalt make these *Medals* or *Pentacles* with exorcised pen and colours, as we shall hereafter show thee. Whensoever thou constructest them, if thou canst complete them in the hour wherein thou didst begin them, it is better. However, if it be absolutely necessary to interrupt the work, thou shouldest await the proper day and hour before re-commencing it.

The *Pentacles* being finished and completed, take a cloth of very fine silk, as we shall hereafter ordain thee, in the which thou shalt wrap the Pentacles. After which thou shalt take a large Vessel of Earth filled with Charcoal, upon the which there must be put frankincense, mastic, and aloes, all having been previously conjured and exorcised as shall hereafter be told thee. Thou must also be thyself pure, clean, and washed, as thou shalt find given in the proper place. Furthermore, thou shouldest have the Sickle or Knife of Magical Art, with the which thou shalt make a Circle, and trace within it an inner circle, and in the space between the

* *i.e.* in Gemini, Libra, Aquarius, Taurus, Virgo, or Capricorn.

two thou shalt write the Names of God,* which thou shalt think fit and proper. It is necessary after this that thou shouldest have within the Circle a vessel of earth with burning coals and odoriferous perfumes thereon; with the which thou shalt fumigate the aforesaid *Pentacles;* and, having turned thy face towards the East, thou shalt hold the said *Pentacles* over the smoke of the *Temple Incense,* and shalt repeat devoutly the following *Psalms* of *David* my *Father: Psalms* viii., xxi., xxvii., xxix., xxxii., li., lxxii., cxxxiv.†

(For a convenient form of Circle which may be used for preparing Instruments and other things of the same kind, as well as for consecrating the *Pentacles, see Figure* 3.)

After this thou shalt repeat the following Oration:—

THE ORATION.

O ADONAI most powerful, EL most strong, AGLA most holy, ON most righteous, the ALEPH‡ and the TAU, the Beginning and the End; Thou Who hast established all things in Thy Wisdom; Thou Who has chosen Abraham Thy faithful servant, and hast promised that in his seed shall all nations of the earth be blessed, which seed Thou hast multiplied as the Stars of Heaven; Thou Who hast appeared unto Thy servant Moses in flame in the midst of the *Burning Bush,* and hast made him walk with dry feet through the Red Sea; Thou Who gavest the Law to him upon Mount Sinai; Thou Who hast granted unto SOLOMON Thy Servant these *Pentacles* by Thy great Mercy, for the preservation of Soul and of Body; we most humbly implore and supplicate Thy Holy Majesty, that these *Pentacles* may be consecrated by Thy power, and prepared in such manner that they may obtain virtue and strength against all Spirits, through Thee, O Most Holy ADONAI, Whose Kingdom, Empire, and principality, remaineth and endureth without end.

These words being said, thou shalt perfume the *Pentacles* with the same sweet scents and perfumes, and afterwards having wrapped them in a piece of prepared silk cloth, thou shalt put them in a place fit and clean, which thou mayest open whenever it shall please thee, and close it again, at thy pleasure and according unto thy will. We will hereafter show thee the method and manner of preparing the aforesaid place, of perfuming it with scents and sweet odours, and of sprinkling it with the Water and *Water-Sprinkler* of *Magical Art;* for all these things contain many good properties, and innumerable virtues, as experience will easily teach thee.

We have already said sufficient regarding the *Solemn Conjuration of Spirits.*

We have also spoken enough in our present Key, regarding the manner in which it is necessary to attract the Spirits so as to make them speak. Now, by Divine aid, I will teach thee how to perform certain experiments with success.

* Preferably those having some reference to the work in hand.

† I have given the number of the Psalms according to the *English,* not the *Hebrew* numbers.

‡ The Qabalistic word AZOTH may be substituted for "the Aleph and the Tau."

Know,* O my Son Roboam, that all the Divine Sigils, Characters, and Names (which are the most precious and excellent things in Nature, whether Terrestrial or Celestial), should be written by thee each separately, when thou art in a state of grace and purity, upon Virgin parchment, with ordinary ink, in the beginning of the month† of August before sunrise, raising thine eyes unto heaven, and turning towards the east. Thou shalt preserve them to suspend from thy neck, whichever thou wilt, on the day and hour wherein thou wast born, after which thou shalt take heed to name every day ten times, the Name which is hung from thy neck, turning towards the East, and thou mayest be assured that no enchantment or any other danger shall have power to harm thee.

Furthermore thou shalt vanquish all adversities, and shalt be cherished and loved by the Angels and Spirits, provided that thou hast made their characters and that thou hast them upon thee; I assure thee that this is the true way to succeed with ease in all thine operations, for being fortified with a Divine Name, and the Letters, Characters, and *Sigils*, applicable unto the operation, thou shalt discover with what supernatural exactitude and very great promptitude, both Terrestrial and Celestial things will be obedient unto thee. But all this will only be true, when accompanied by the Pentacles which hereinafter follow, seeing that the Seals, Characters, and Divine Names, serve only to fortify the work, to preserve from unforeseen accidents, and to attract the familiarity of the Angels and Spirits; which is one reason, my Son, that before making any experiment, I order thee to read and re-read my Testament, not once only but many times, so that being perfectly instructed in the several Ceremonies thou mayest in no way fail, and that thus what shall have previously appeared to thee difficult and lengthy, may become in process of time easy and of very great use.

I am about to endow thee with many secrets, which I charge thee never to employ for an evil purpose, for ACCURSED BE HE WHO TAKETH THE NAME OF ALMIGHTY GOD IN VAIN; but thou mayest without any other ceremonies make use of them, provided that, as I have already said, thou hast only the Glory of Eternal God for thine object. Thus, after having taught thee all the Ceremonies which concern the manner of performing the Operations, I am at length determined to make thee a partaker in the secrets of which I have particular knowledge, unknown to this day unto the generality of men; but, nevertheless, only on the condition that thou attemptest not the ruin and destruction of thy neighbour, for his blood will cry for vengeance unto God, and in the end thou and thine shall feel the just wrath of an offended Deity. However, God not having forbidden honest and lawful pleasures, thou mayest perform boldly the Operations which follow, it being always especially necessary to distinguish between the good and the evil, so as to choose the former and avoid the latter, which is why I command thee to be attentive to all that is contained in this my Testament.

* From here to the end of the Chapter is only given in Lansdowne MSS. 1203.
† *i.e.* When the Sun is in the Sign Leo.

BOOK ONE.

CHAPTER IX.

Of the Experiment Concerning Things Stolen, and How It Should Be Performed.

My beloved Son, if thou findest any Theft, thou shalt do as is hereinafter ordained, and with the help of God thou shalt find that which hath been taken away.

If the hours and days be not otherwise ordained in this operation, thou must refer to what hath already been said. But before commencing any operation whatsoever for the recovery of things stolen, after having made all necessary preparations, thou shalt say the following Oration:—

THE ORATION.

Ateh Adonai Elohim Asher Ha-Shamain Ve-Ha-Aretz, &c.*

Thou, O Lord, Who hast made both Heaven and Earth, and hast measured them in the hollow of Thy hand; Thou Who art seated upon the Kerubim and the Seraphim, in the high places, whereunto human understanding cannot penetrate; Thou Who hast created all things by Thine agency, in Whose Presence are the Living Creatures, of which four are marvellously volatile, which have six wings, and who incessantly cry aloud: "Qadosch, Qadosch, Qadosch, Adonai Elohim Tzabaoth, Heaven and Earth are full of Thy Glory;" O Lord God, Thou Who hast expelled Adam from the Terrestrial Paradise, and Who hast placed the Kerubim to guard the Tree of Life, Thou art the Lord Who alone doest wonders; show forth I pray Thee Thy Great Mercy, by the Holy City of Jerusalem, by Thy wonderful Name of four letters which are Yod, He, Vau, He, and by Thy Holy and Admirable Name, give unto me the power and virtue to enable me to accomplish this experiment, and to come unto the desired end of this operation; through Thee Who art Life, and unto Whom Life belongeth unto the eternal ages. Amen.

After this perfume and cense the place by burning *Temple Incense.* This aforesaid place should be pure, clean, safe from interruption or disturbance, and proper to the work, as we shall hereafter show. Then sprinkle the aforesaid place with consecrated Water, as is laid down in the *Chapter concerning Circles.*

The Operation being in such wise prepared, thou shalt rehearse the Conjuration necessary for this experiment, at the end of which Thou shalt say as follows:—

* This is simply the Hebrew of the prayer which follows; but in the MS. Codices it is so mutilated as to be worthless.

O Almighty Father and Lord, Who regardest the Heavens, the Earth, and the Abyss, mercifully grant unto me by Thy Holy Name written with four letters, YOD, HE, VAU, HE, that by this exorcism I may obtain virtue, Thou Who art IAH, IAH, IAH, grant that by Thy power these Spirits may discover that which we require and which we hope to find, and may they show and declare unto us the persons who have committed the theft, and where they are to be found.

I conjure ye, over this burning Temple Incense, anew, ye Spirits above named, by all the aforesaid Names, through which all things created tremble, that ye show openly unto me (or unto this child here present with us*) those things which we seek.

These things being accomplished they will make thee to see plainly that which thou seekest. Take note that the Exorcist, or Master of the Art, should be such as is ordained in the Chapter concerning the Exorcist and his Companions; and if in this experiment it should be necessary to write down characters or Names, thou shalt do that which it is necessary to observe regarding the pen, ink, and paper, as is duly prescribed in the chapters concerning them.

For if thou dost not regard these things, thou wilt neither accomplish that which thou desirest, nor arrive at thy desired end.

HOW TO KNOW WHO HAS COMMITTED A THEFT‡

Take a Sieve, after burning one-half teaspoonful of *Temple Incense*, and suspend it by a piece of cord wherewith a man has been hung, which should be fastened round the circumference of the rim Within the rim write with blood in the four divisions thereof the characters given in *Figure* 4. After this take a basin of brass perfectly clean which thou shalt fill with water from a fountain, and having pronounced these words: DIES MIES YES-CHET BENE DONE FET DONNIMA METEMAUZ, make the sieve spin round with thy left hand, and at the same time turn with thy right hand the water in the basin in a contrary direction, by stirring it with a twig of green laurel. When the water becometh still and the sieve no longer whirls, gaze fixedly into the water, and thou shalt see the form of him who hath committed the theft; and in order that thou mayest the more easily recognize him, thou shalt mark him in some part of his face with the Magical Sword of Art; for that sign which thou shalt have cut therewith in the water, shall be really found thereafter upon his own person.

THE MANNER OF CAUSING THE SIEVE TO TURN, THAT THOU MAYEST KNOW WHO HAS COMMITTED THE THEFT†

Take a Sieve and stick into the outside of the rim the open points of a pair of scissors, and having rested the rings of the said opened scissors

* A child employed as a clairvoyant in the operation; as is still the custom in some places in the East.

† The rest of this Chapter is from 1203 Lansdowne MSS.

‡ This is the ancient divination by the sieve and shears, and from St. Peter and St. Paul being mentioned in it, has evidently undergone a mediæval reconstruction.

on the thumb-nails of two persons, let one of them say the following Prayer:—

PRAYER.

DIES MIES YES-CHET BENE DONE FET DONNIMA METEMAUZ; O Lord, Who liberatedst the holy Susanna from a false accusation of crime; O Lord, Who liberatedst the holy Thekla; O Lord, Who rescuedst the holy Daniel from the den of lions, and the Three Children from the burning fiery furnace, free the innocent and reveal the guilty.

After this let him or her pronounce aloud the names and surnames of all the persons living in the house where the theft hast been committed, who may be suspected of having stolen the things in question, saying:—

"By Saint Peter and Saint Paul, such a person hath not done this thing."

And let the other reply:—

"By Saint Peter and Saint Paul, he (or she) hath not done it."

Let this be repeated thrice for each person named and suspected, and it is certain that on naming the person who hath committed the theft or done the crime, the sieve will turn of itself without its being able to stop it, and by this thou shalt know the evil doer.

BOOK ONE.

CHAPTER X.

Of the Experiment of Invisibility, and How It Should Be Performed.

If thou wishest to perform the *Experiment of Invisibility*, thou shalt follow the instructions for the same. If it be necessary to observe the day and the hour, thou shalt do as is said in their Chapters. But if thou needest not observe the day and the hour as marked in the Chapter thereon, thou shalt do as taught in the Chapter which precedeth it. If in the course of the experiment it be necessary to write anything, it should be done as is described in the Chapters pertaining thereto, with the proper pen, paper, and ink, or blood. But if the matter is to be accomplished by invocation, before thy conjurations, thou shalt, while burning *Temple Incense*, say devoutly in thine heart:—

Sceaboles, Arbaron, Elohi, Elimigith, Herenobulcule, Methe, Baluth, Timayal, Villaquiel, Teveni, Yevie, Ferete, Bacuhaba, Guvarin; through Him by Whom ye have empire and power over men, ye must accomplish this work so that I may go and remain invisible.

And if it be necessary in this operation to trace a Circle, thou shalt do as is ordained in the Chapter concerning Circles; and if it be necessary to write Characters, &c., thou shalt follow the instructions given in the respective Chapters.

This operation being thus prepared, if there be an especial Conjuration to perform, thou shalt repeat it in the proper manner; if not, thou shalt say the general Conjuration, at the end of which thou shalt add the following words:

O thou Almiras, Master of Invisibility, with thy Ministers Cheros, Maitor, Tangedem, Transidim, Suvantos, Abelaios, Bored, Belamith, Castumi, Dabuel; I conjure ye by Him Who maketh Earth and Heaven to tremble, Who is seated upon the Throne of His Majesty, that this operation may be perfectly accomplished according to my will, so that at whatsoever time it may please me, I may be able to be invisible.

I conjure thee anew, O Almiras, *Chief of Invisibility*, both thee and thy Ministers, by Him through Whom all things have their being, and by Saturiel, Harchiel, Daniel, Beniel, Assimonem, that thou immediately comest thither with all thy Ministers, and achievest this operation, as thou knowest it ought to be accomplished, and that by the same operation thou render me invisible, so that none may be able to see me.

In order then to accomplish this aforesaid operation, thou must prepare all things necessary with requisite care and diligence, and put them in practice with all the general and particular ceremonies laid down for these experiments; and with all the conditions contained in our first and second Books. Thou shalt also in the same operations duly repeat the appropriate Conjurations, with all the solemnities marked in the respective Chapters. Thus shalt thou accomplish the experiment surely and without hindrance, and thus shalt thou find it true.

But, on the contrary, if thou lettest any of these things escape thee, or if thou despiseth them, never shalt thou be able to arrive at thy proposed end; as, for example, we enter not easily into a fenced city over its walls but through its gates.

HOW* TO RENDER ONESELF INVISIBLE.

Make a small image of yellow wax, in the form of a man, in the month January and in the day and hour of Saturn, and at that time write with a needle above the crown of its head and upon its skull which thou shalt have adroitly raised, the character following. (*See Figure* 5.) After which thou shalt re-place the skull in proper position. Thou shalt then write upon a small strip of the skin of a frog or toad which thou shalt have killed, the following words and characters. (*See Figure* 6.) Thou shalt then go and suspend the said figure by one of thy hairs from the vault of a cavern at the hour of midnight, and burning *Temple Incense* under it, thou shalt say:—

METATRON, MELEKH, BEROTH, NOTH, VENIBBETH, MACH, and all ye, I conjure thee O Figure of wax, by the Living God, that by the virtue of these Characters and words, thou render me invisible, wherever I may bear thee with me. Amen.

And after having burned *Temple Incense* again under it, thou shalt bury it in the same place in a small deal box, and every time that thou wishest to pass or enter into any place without being seen, thou shalt say these words, bearing the aforesaid figure in thy left pocket:—

Come unto me and never quit me whithersoever I shall go.

Afterwards thou shalt take it carefully back unto the before-mentioned place and cover it with earth until thou shalt need it again.

* The rest of this Chapter is from 1203 Lansdowne MSS.

BOOK ONE.

CHAPTER XI.

To Hinder a Sportsman from Killing Any Game.

Take a stick of green elder, from the two ends of which thou shalt clean out the pith.* In each end place a strip of parchment of hare-skin, having written thereon with the blood of a black hen the following character and word. (*See Figure* 7.) Having made two of these slips, place one in each end of the stick and close the apertures up with pith, afterwards on a Friday in the month of February thou shalt fumigate the aforesaid stick with suitable incense thrice in the air, and having taken it thence thou shalt bury it in the earth under an elder tree. Afterwards thou shalt expose it in the pathway by which the Sportsman will pass, and once he has passed by it, he need not hope to kill any game during that day. If thou shalt wish a second time to lay a spell upon him in like manner, thou needest but to expose the stick again in his path; but take care to bury it again in the earth under an elder tree, so as to be able to take it from thence each time that thou shalt have need of it; and to take it up each time as soon as the Sportsman shall have passed.

* This Chapter is taken from 1203 Lansdowne MSS.

BOOK ONE.

CHAPTER XII.

How to Make the Magic Garters.

TAKE enough of the skin of a stag to make two hollow tubular Garters,* but before stitching them up thou shalt write on the side of the skin which was next the flesh the words and characters shown in *Figure* 8, with the blood of a hare killed on the 25th of June, and having filled the said Garters with green mugwort gathered also on the 25th of June before sunrise, thou shalt put in the two ends of each the eye of the fish called barbel; and when thou shalt wish to use them thou shalt get up before sunrise and wash them in a brook of running water, and place them one on each leg above the knee. After this thou shalt take a short rod of holm-oak cut on the same 25th of June, turn in the direction thou wishest to go, write upon the ground the name of the place, and commencing thy journey thou wilt find it accomplished in a few days and without fatigue. When thou wishest to stop thou hast only to say AMECH and beat the air with the aforesaid wand, and incontinently thou shalt be on firm ground.

* This Chapter is also taken from 1203 Lansdowne MSS.

BOOK ONE.

CHAPTER XIII.

HOW TO MAKE THE MAGIC CARPET PROPER FOR INTERROGATING THE INTELLIGENCES, SO AS TO OBTAIN AN ANSWER REGARDING WHATSOEVER MATTER ONE MAY WISH TO LEARN.

MAKE a Carpet* of white and new wool, and when the Moon shall be at her full, in the Sign of Capricorn and in the hour of the Sun, thou shalt go into the country away from any habitation of man, in a place free from all impurity, and shalt spread out thy Carpet so that one of its points shall be towards the east, and another towards the west, and having made a Circle without it and enclosing it, thou shalt remain within upon the point towards the east, and holding thy wand in the air for every operation, thou shalt call upon MICHAEL,† towards the north upon RAPHAEL, towards the west upon GABRIEL, and towards the south upon MURIEL. After this thou shalt return unto the point of the East and devoutly invoke the Great Name AGLA, and take this point of the Carpet in thy left hand; turning then towards the North thou shalt do the same, and so continuing to the other points of the Carpet, thou shalt raise them so that they touch not the ground, and holding them up thus, and turning anew towards the East thou shalt say with great veneration the following Prayer:—

PRAYER.

AGLA, AGLA, AGLA, AGLA; O God Almighty Who art the Life of the Universe and Who rulest over the four divisions of its vast form by the strength and virtue of the Four Letters of Thy Holy Name Tetragrammaton, YOD, HE, VAU, HE, bless in Thy Name this covering which I hold as Thou hast blessed the Mantle of Elijah in the hands of Elisha, so that being covered by Thy Wings, nothing may be able to injure me, even as it is said:—"He shall hide thee under His Wings and beneath His feathers shall thou trust, His truth shall be thy shield and buckler."

After this thou shalt fold it up, saying these words following:—RECABUSTIRA, CABUSTIRA, BUSTIRA, TIRA RA, A; and shall keep it carefully to serve thee at need.

When thou shalt be desirous to make thine interrogations, choose the night of full or of new moon, and from midnight until daybreak.

* This Chapter is also taken from 1203 Lansdowne MSS.

† I have usually found Michael attributed to the South; Raphael to the East; Gabriel to the West; and Auriel to the North. Likewise I think the operator should turn following the course of the Sun, and not contrariwise as in the text.

Thou shalt transport thyself unto the appointed spot if it be for the purpose of discovering a treasure; if not, any place will serve provided it be clean and pure. Having had the precaution on the preceding evening to write upon a slip of virgin parchment coloured azure-blue, with a pen made from the feather of a dove, this Character and Name (*see Figure* 9); taking thy carpet, thou shalt cover thy head and body therewith, and taking the censer, with new fire therein, thou shalt place it in or upon the proper place, and cast thereon some incense. Then shalt thou prostrate thyself upon the ground, with thy face towards the earth, before the incense beginneth to fume, keeping the fire of the same beneath the carpet, holding thy wand upright, against which to rest thy chin; thou shalt hold with thy right hand the aforesaid strip of parchment against thy forehead, and thou shalt say the following words:—

VEGALE, HAMICATA, UMSA, TERATA, YEH, DAH, MA, BAXASOXA, UN, HORAH, HIMESERE; O God the Vast One send unto me the Inspiration of Thy Light, make me to discover the secret thing which I ask of Thee, whatsoever such or such a thing may be, make me to search it out by the aid of Thy holy Ministers RAZIEL, TZAPHNIEL, MATMONIEL; Lo, Thou hast desired truth in the young, and in the hidden thing shalt Thou make me known wisdom. RECABUSTIRA, CABUSTIRA, BUSTIRA, TIRA, RA, A, KARKAHITA, KAHITA, HITA, TA.

And thou shalt hear distinctly the answer which thou shalt have sought.

BOOK ONE.

CHAPTER XIV.

How to Render Thyself Master of a Treasure Possessed by the Spirits.

The Earth being inhabited, as I have before said unto thee, by a great number of Celestial Beings and Spirits,* who by their subtilty and prevision know the places wherein treasures are hidden, and seeing that it often happenneth that those men who undertake a search for these said treasures are molested and sometimes put to death by the aforesaid Spirits, which are called Gnomes; which, however, is not done through the Avarice of these said Gnomes, a Spirit being incapable of possessing anything, having no material senses wherewith to bring it into use, but because these Spirits, who are enemies of the passions, are equally so of Avarice, unto which men are so much inclined; and foreseeing the evil ends for which these treasures will be employed have some interest and aim in maintaining the earth in its condition of price and value, seeing that they are its inhabitants, and when they slightly disturb the workers in such kind of treasures, it is a warning which they give them to cease from the work, and if it happen that the greedy importunity of the aforesaid workers oblige them to continue, notwithstanding the aforesaid warnings, the Spirits, irritated by their despising the same, frequently put the workmen to death. But know, O my Son, that from the time that thou shalt have the good fortune to be familiar with such kinds of Spirits, and that thou shalt be able by means of what I have taught thee to make them submit unto thine orders, they will be happy to give thee, and to make thee partaker in that which they uselessly possess, provided that thine object and end shall be to make a good use thereof.

THE MANNER OF PERFORMING THE OPERATION.

On a Sunday before sunrise, between the 10th of July and the 20th of August, when the moon is in the Sign of the Lion, thou shalt go unto the place where thou shalt know either by interrogation of the Intelligences, or otherwise, that there is a treasure; there thou shalt describe a Circle of sufficient size with the Sword of Magical Art wherein to open up the earth, as the nature of the ground will allow; thrice during the day shalt thou cense it with the incense proper for the day, after which being clothed in the raiment proper for the Operation thou shalt suspend in some way by a machine immediately above the opening a lamp, whose oil should be mingled with the fat of a man who has died in the month of July, and the

* This is also taken from 1203 Lansdowne MSS.

wick being made from the cloth wherein he has been buried. Having kindled this with fresh fire, thou shalt fortify the workmen with a girdle of the skin of a goat newly slain, whereon shall be written with the blood of the dead man from whom thou shalt have taken the fat these words and characters (*see Figure* 10); and thou shalt set them to work in safety, warning them not to be at all disturbed at the Spectres which they will see, but to work away boldly. In case they cannot finish the work in a single day, every time they shall have to leave it thou shalt cause them to put a covering of wood over the opening, and above the covering about six inches of earth; and thus shalt thou continue unto the end, being all the time present in the raiment of the Art, and with the Magic Sword, during the operation. After which thou shalt repeat this prayer:—

PRAYER.

ADONAI, ELOHIM, EL, EHEIEH ASHER EHEIEH, Prince of Princes, Existence of Existences, have mercy upon me, and cast Thine eyes upon Thy Servant (N.), who invokes Thee most devoutedly, and supplicates Thee by Thy Holy and tremendous Name *Tetragrammaton* to be propitious, and to order Thine Angels and Spirits to come and take up their abode in this place; O ye Angels and Spirits of the Stars, O all ye Angels and Elementary Spirits, O all ye Spirits present before the Face of God, I the Minister and faithful Servant of the Most High conjure ye, let God himself, the Existence of Existences, conjure ye to come and be present at this Operation, I, the Servant of God, most humbly entreat ye. Amen.

Having then caused the workmen to fill in the hole, thou shalt license the Spirits to depart, thanking them for the favour they have shown unto thee, and saying:—

THE LICENSE TO DEPART.

O ye good and happy Spirits, we thank ye for the benefits which we have just received from your liberal bounty; depart ye in peace to govern the Element which God hath destined for your habitation. Amen.

BOOK ONE.

CHAPTER XV.

Of the Experiment of Seeking Favour and Love.

If thou wishest to perform the Experiment of seeking favor and love,* observe in what manner the Experiment is to be carried out, and if it be dependent upon the day and the hour, perform it in the day and the hour required, as thou wilt find it in the chapter concerning the hours; and if the Experiment be one that requireth writing, thou shalt write as it is said in the chapter concerning the same; and if it be with penal bonds, pacts, and fumigations, then thou shalt cense with a fit perfume as is said in the chapter concerning suffumigations; and if it be necessary to sprinkle it with water and hyssop, then let it be as in the chapter concerning the same; similarly if such Experiment require characters, names, or the like, let such names be written as the chapter concerning the writing of characters, and place the same in a clean place as hath been said. Then thou shalt repeat over it, after burning Temple Incense, the following Oration:—

THE ORATION.

O Adonai, most Holy, Most Righteous, and most Mighty God, Who hast made all things through Thy Mercy and Righteousness wherewith Thou art filled, grant unto us that we may be found worthy that this Experiment may be found consecrated and perfect, so that the Light may issue from Thy Most Holy Seat, O Adonai, which may obtain for us favor and love. Amen.

This being said, thou shalt place it in clean silk, and bury it for a day and a night at the junction of four cross-roads; and whensoever thou wishest to obtain any grace or favor from any, take it, having first properly consecrated it according to the rule, and place it in thy right hand, and seek thou what thou wilt it shall not be denied thee. But if thou doest not the Experiment carefully and rightly, assuredly thou shalt not succeed in any manner.

For obtaining grace and love write down the following words:—

Sator,† Arepo, Tenet, Opera, Rotas, Iah, Iah, Iah, Enam, Iah, Iah, Iah, Kether, Chokmah, Binah, Gedulah, Geburah, Tiphereth, Netzach, Hod, Yesod, Malkuth, Abraham, Isaac, Jacob, Shadrach, Meshach, Abednego, be ye all present in my aid and for whatsoever I shall desire to obtain.

Which words being properly written as above, thou shalt also find thy desire brought to pass.

* This Chapter is taken from 10,862 Add. MSS.

† This Incantation is also given in 1307 Sloane MSS., page 76.

BOOK ONE.

CHAPTER XVI.

How Operations of Mockery, Invisibility, and Deceit Should Be Prepared.

Experiments relating to tricks, mockeries, and deceits, may be performed in many ways.* When thou shalt wish to practice these experiments with regard to any person, thou shalt observe the day and the hour as we have already said. Should it be necessary to write Characters or Words, it should be done on *Virgin Parchment Paper*, as we shall show farther on. As for the ink, if it be not specially ordained in this operation, it is advisable to use the blood of a bat with the pen and the needle of art. But before describing or writing the Characters or Names, all the necessary rules should be observed as given in the proper Chapters, and having carefully followed out all these, thou shalt pronounce with a loud voice the following words:—

Abac, Aldal, Iat, Hudac, Guthac, Guthor, Gomeh, Tistator, Derisor, Destatur, come hither all ye who love the times and places wherein all kinds of mockeries and deceits are practiced. And ye who make things disappear and who render them invisible, come hither to deceive all those who regard these things, so that they may be deceived, and that they may seem to see that which they see not and hear that which they hear not, so that their senses may be deceived, and that they may behold that which is not true.

Come ye then hither and remain, and consecrate this enchantment, seeing that God the Almighty Lord hath destined ye for such.

When this Experiment is completed in this manner in the hour and time which we have shown and taught, also the foregoing words Abac, Aldal, &c., should be written with the pen as hereinafter ordained; but if the Experiment be performed in a different way, yet shalt thou always say the aforesaid words, and they should be repeated as before given.

If thou practicest these things in this manner correctly, thou shalt arrive at the effect of thine operations and experiments, by the which thou mayest easily deceive the senses.

* This Chapter is given in 10862 Add. MSS. 3981 Harleian MSS., 288 King's MSS., 3091 Sloane MSS., and 1307 Sloane MSS., but is wanting in 1202 Lansdowne MSS., as are all the Chapters of the First Book after Chap. 8.

BOOK ONE.

CHAPTER XVII.

How Extraordinary Experiments and Operations Should Be Prepared.

We have spoken in the preceding Chapters of common experiments and operations, which it is more usual to practice and put in operation, and therein thou mayest easily see that we have told thee sufficient for their perfection. In this Chapter we treat of extraordinary and unusual experiments, which can also be done in many ways.

None the less should those who wish to put in practice the like experiments and operations observe the days and hours as is laid down in the proper Chapters, and should be provided with *Genuine Parchment* Paper, made from the skin of dead-born Lambs*, and other necessary things. Having prepared a similar experiment thou shalt say:—

PRAYER.

O God, Who hast created all things, and hast given unto us discernment to understand the good and the evil; through thy Holy Name, and through these Holy Names;—Iod, Iah, Vau, Daleth, Vau, Tzabaoth, Zio, Amator, Creator, do Thou, O Lord, grant that this experiment may become true and veritable in my hands through Thy Holy Seal, O Adonai, Whose reign and empire remaineth eternally and unto the Ages of the Ages. Amen.

This being done, thou shalt perform the experiment, observing its hour, and thou shalt perfume and incense as is laid down in the proper Chapter; sprinkling with exorcised water, and performing all the ceremonies and solemnities as we shall instruct thee in the Second Book of our Key.

BOOK ONE.

CHAPTER XVIII.

Concerning the Holy Pentacles or Medals.

The *Medals or Pentacles,* which we make for the purpose of striking terror into the Spirits and reducing them to obedience, have besides this wonderful and excellent virtue. If thou invokest the Spirits by virtue of these *Pentacles,* they will obey thee without repugnance, and having considered them they will be struck with astonishment, and will fear them, and thou shalt see them so surprised by fear and terror, that none of them will be sufficiently bold to wish to oppose thy will. They are also of great virtue and efficacy against all perils of Earth, of Air, of Water, and of Fire, against poison which hath been drunk, against all kinds of infirmities and necessities, against binding, sortilege, and sorcery, against all terror and fear, and wheresoever thou shalt find thyself, if armed with them, thou shalt be in safety all the days of thy life.

Through them do we acquire grace and good-will from man and woman, fire is extinguished, water is stayed, and all Creatures fear at the sight of the Names which are therein, and obey through that fear.

These *Pentacles* are usually made of the metal the most suitable to the nature of the Planet; and then there is no occasion to observe the rule of particular colors. They should be engraved with the instrument of Art in the days and hours proper to the Planet.

Saturn ruleth over Lead; Jupiter over Tin; Mars over Iron; the Sun over Gold; Venus over Copper; Mercury over the mixture of Metals; and the Moon over Silver.

They may also be made with *Virgin Parchment* paper, writing thereon with the colors adopted for each Planet, referring to the rules already laid down in the proper Chapters, and according to the Planet with which the Pentacle is in sympathy.

Wherefore unto Saturn the color of Black is appropriated; Jupiter ruleth over Celestial Blue; Mars over Red; the Gun over Gold, or the color of Yellow or Citron; Venus over Green; Mercury over Mixed Colors; the Moon over Silver, or the color of Argentine Earth.

The Matter of which the *Pentacle* is constructed should be Virgin, never having been used for any other purpose; or if it be metal it should be purified by fire.

As regards the size of the *Pentacles* it is arbitrary, so long as they are made according to the rules, and with the requisite solemnities, as hath been ordained.

The* virtues of the *Holy Pentacles* are no less advantageous unto thee than the knowledge of the secrets which I have already given unto thee; and thou shouldst take particular care if thou makest them upon virgin parchment to use the proper colors; and if thou engravest them

* This and the four following paragraphs are from 1203 Lansdowne MSS.

upon metal, to do so in the manner taught thee; and so shalt thou have the satisfaction of seeing them produce the promised effect. But seeing that this Science is not a Science of argument and open reasoning, but that, on the contrary, it is entirely mysterious and occult, we should not argue and deliberate over these matters, and it is sufficient to believe firmly to enable us to bring into operation that which hath already been taught.

When thou shalt construct these *Pentacles* and *Characters*, it is necessary never to forget the burning of *Temple Incense*, nor to employ anything beyond that which hath already been taught.

It is necessary, above all things, to be attentive to the operation, and never to forget or omit those things which contribute to the success which the *Pentacles* and Experiments promise, having ever in thy mind no other intention than the Glory of God, the accomplishment of thy desires, and loving kindness towards thy neighbor.

Furthermore, my beloved Son, I order thee not to bury this Science, but to make thy friends partakers in the same, subject, however, to the strict command never to profane the things which are Divine, for if thou doest this, far from rendering thee a friend of the Spirits, it will but be the means of bringing thee unto destruction.

But never must thou lavish these things among the ignorant, for that would be as blameable as to cast precious gems before swine; on the contrary, from one Sage the secret knowledge should pass unto another Sage, for in this manner shall the Treasure of Treasures never descend into oblivion.

Adore* and revere the Most Holy Names of God which are found in these *Pentacles* and Characters, for without this never shalt thou be able to come to the end of any enterprise, nor to accomplish the *Mystery of Mysteries*.

Above all things, remember that to perform any of these operations thou must be pure in body and mind, and without blemish, and omit not any of the preparations.

This Key, full of Mysteries, hath been revealed unto me by an Angel.

Accursed be he who undertaketh our Art without having the qualities requisite to thoroughly understand our "*Key*," accursed be he who invoketh the Name of God in vain, for such an one prepareth for himself the punishments which await the unbelievers, for God shall abandon them and relegate them unto the depths of Hell amongst the impure Spirits.

For God is great and Immutable, He hath been for ever, and He shall remain even unto the end of the Ages.

ACCURSED BE HE WHO TAKETH THE NAME OF GOD IN VAIN! ACCURSED BE HE WHO USETH THIS KNOWLEDGE UNTO AN EVIL END, BE HE ACCURSED IN THIS WORLD AND IN THE WORLD TO COME. AMEN. BE HE ACCURSED IN THE NAME WHICH HE HATH BLASPHEMED!

* The rest of the Chapter is from 1202 Lansdowne MSS., except the last sentence.

THE END OF THE FIRST BOOK.

HERE FOLLOW THE HOLY PENTACLES, EXPRESSED IN THEIR PROPER FIGURES AND CHARACTERS, TOGETHER WITH THEIR ESPECIAL VIRTUES; FOR THE USE OF THE MASTER OF ART.

THE ORDER OF THE PENTACLES.

(1) Seven Pentacles consecrated to Saturn=Black.
(2) Seven Pentacles consecrated to Jupiter=Blue.
(3) Seven Pentacles consecrated to Mars=Red.
(4) Seven Pentacles consecrated to the Sun=Yellow.
(5) Five Pentacles consecrated to Venus=Green.
(6) Five Pentacles consecrated to Mercury=Mixed Colors.
(7) Six Pentacles consecrated to the Moon=Silver.

Editor's Note on Figure 1.—The Mystical Figure of SOLOMON.—This is only given in the two MSS., Lansdowne 1202 and 1203. It was given by Lévi in his "*Dogme et Rituel de la Haute Magie,*" and by *Tycho Brahé* in his "*Calendarium Naturale Magicum,*" but in each instance without the Hebrew words and letters, probably because these were so mangled by illiterate transcribers as to be unrecognizable. After much labor and study of the figure, I believe the words in the body of the symbol to be intended for the *Ten Sephiroth* arranged in the form of the *Tree of Life,* with the Name of SOLOMON to the right and to the left; while the surrounding characters are intended for the twenty-two letters of the *Hebrew Alphabet.* I have, therefore, thus restored them. This Figure forms in each instance the frontispiece of the MS. referred to.

SATURN.

Figure 11.—The First Pentacle of Saturn.—This *Pentacle* is of great value and utility for striking terror into the Spirits. Wherefore, upon its being shown to them they submit, and kneeling upon the earth before it, they obey.

Editor's Note.—The Hebrew Letters within the square are the four great Names of God which are written with four letters:—IHVH, Yod,

PLATE II.

Fig. 6.

Fig. 7.

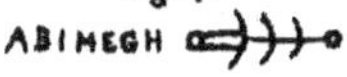

Fig. 8.

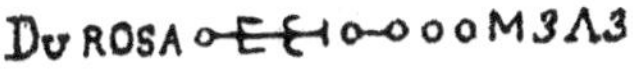

Fig. 9.

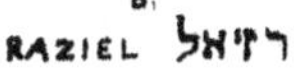

Fig. 10.

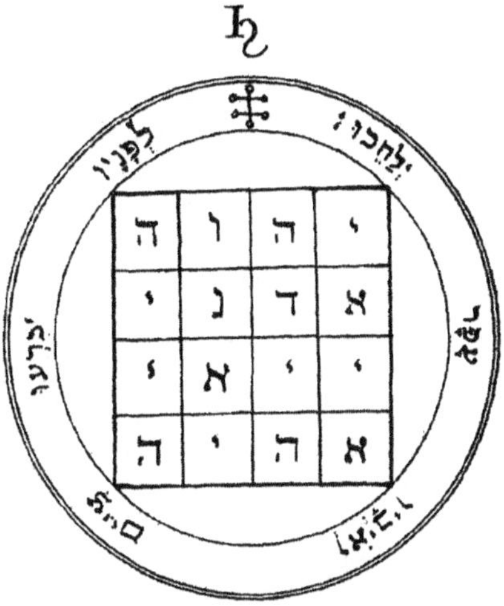

Fig. 11.

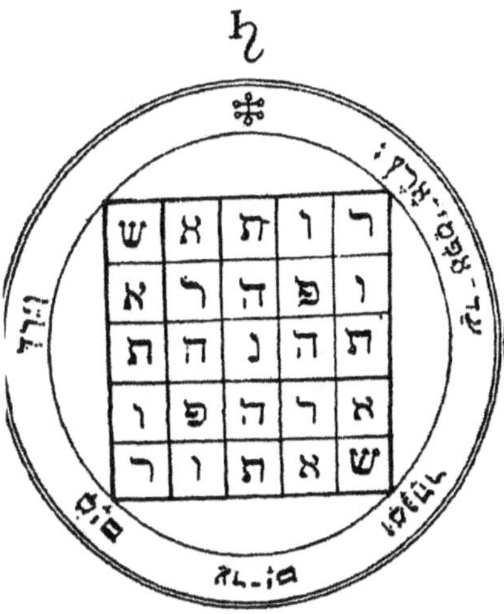

Fig. 12.

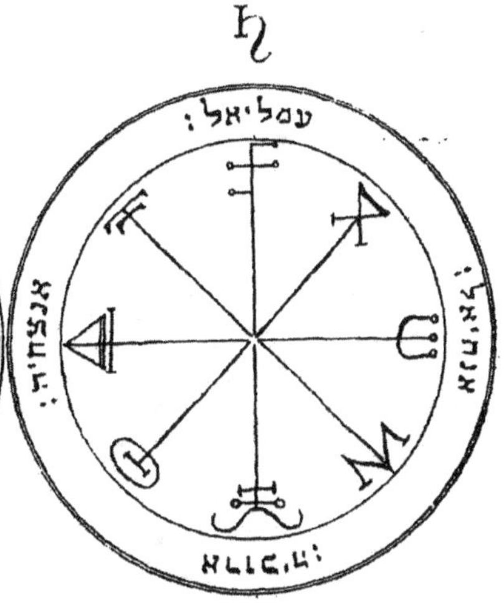

Fig. 13.

PLATE III

Fig. 14.

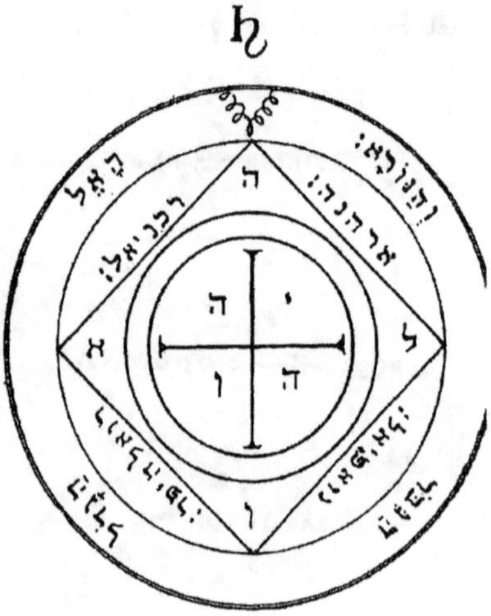

Fig. 15.

Fig. 16.

Fig. 17.

He, Vau, He; ADNI, Adonai; IIAI, Yiai (this Name has the same Numerical value in Hebrew as the Name El); and AHIH, Eheieh. The Hebrew versicle which surrounds it is from *Psalm lxxii.* 9; "The *Ethiopians* shall kneel before Him, His enemies shall lick the dust."

Figure 12.—The Second Pentacle of Saturn.—This *Pentacle* is of great value against adversaries; and of especial use in repressing the pride of the Spirits.

Editor's Note.—This is the celebrated

SATOR
AREPO
TENET
OPERA
ROTAS,

the most perfect existing form of double acrostic, as far as the arrangement of the letters is concerned; it is repeatedly mentioned in the records of mediæval Magic; and, save to very few, its derivation from the present *Pentacle* has been unknown. It will be seen at a glance that it is a square of five, giving twenty-five letters, which, added to the unity, gives twenty-six, the numerical value of IHVH. The Hebrew versicle surrounding it is taken from *Psalm lxxii.* 8, "His dominion shall be also from the one sea to the other, and from the flood unto the world's end." This passage consists also of exactly twenty-five letters, and its total numerical value (considering the final letters with increased numbers), added to that of the *Name Elohim*, is exactly equal to the total numerical value of the twenty-five letters in the Square.

Figure 13.—The Third Pentacle of Saturn.—This should be made within the *Magical Circle*, and it is good for use at night when thou invokest the Spirits of the nature of Saturn.

Editor's Note.—The characters at the ends of the rays of the Mystic Wheel are Magical Characters of Saturn. Surrounding it are the Names of the Angels:—Omeliel, Anachiel, Arauchiah, and Anazachia, written in Hebrew.

Figure 14.—The Fourth Pentacle of Saturn.—This Pentacle serveth principally for executing all the experiments and operations of ruin, destruction, and death. And when it is made in full perfection, it serveth also for those Spirits which bring news, when thou invokest them from the side of the South.

Editor's Note.—The Hebrew words around the sides of the triangle are from *Deut. vi.* 4:—"Hear, O Israel, IHVH ALHINVH is IHVH ACHD." The surrounding versicle is from *Psalm cix.* 18:—*"As he clothed himself with cursing like as with a garment, so let it come into his bowels like water, and like oil into his bones."* In the center of the *Pentacle* is the mystic letter Yod.

Figure 15.—The Fifth Pentacle of Saturn.—This *Pentacle* defendeth those who invoke the Spirits of Saturn during the night; and chaseth away the Spirits which guard treasures.

Editor's Note.—The Hebrew letters in the angles of the Cross are those of the Name IHVH. Those in the Angles of the Square form ALVH, Eloah. Round the four sides of the Square are the Names of the Angels:—Arehanah, Rakhaniel, Roelhaiphar, and Noaphiel. The versicle is:—"A Great God, a Mighty, and a Terrible."—*Deut. x.* 17.

Figure 16.—The Sixth Pentacle of Saturn.—Around this *Pentacle* is each Name symbolized as it should be. The person against whom thou shalt pronounce it shall be obsessed by Demons.

Editor's Note.—It is formed from Mystical Characters of Saturn. Around it is written in Hebrew: "Set thou a wicked one to be ruler over him, and let Satan stand at his right hand."

Figure 17.—The Seventh and Last Pentacle of Saturn.—This *Pentacle* is fit for exciting earthquakes, seeing that the power of each order of Angels herein invoked is sufficient to make the whole Universe tremble.

Editor's Note.—Within the *Pentacle* are the Names of the Nine Orders of Angels, those of six of them in ordinary Hebrew Characters, and the remainder in the letters which are known as *"The Passing of the River."* These Nine Orders are:—1, CHAIOTH HA-QADESCH, Holy Living Creatures; 2, AUPHANIM, Wheels; 3, ARALIM, Thrones; 4, CHASCHMALIM, Brilliant Ones; 5, SERAPHIM, Fiery Ones; 6, MELAKIM, Kings; 7, ELOHIM, Gods; 8, BENI ELOHIM, Sons of the Elohim; 9,

KERUBIM, Kerubim. The versicle is from *Psalm xviii.* 7:—"Then the earth shook and trembled, the foundations of the hills also moved and were shaken, because He was wroth."

JUPITER.

Figure 18.—The First Pentacle of Jupiter.—This serveth to invoke the Spirits of Jupiter, and especially those whose Names are written around the *Pentacle,* among whom Parasiel is the Lord and Master of Treasures, and teacheth how to become possessor of places wherein they are.

Editor's Note.—This *Pentacle* is composed of Mystical Characters of Jupiter. Around it are the Names of the Angels:—Netoniel, Devachiah, Tzedeqiah, and Parasiel, written in Hebrew.

Figure 19.—The Second Pentacle of Jupiter.—This is proper for acquiring glory, honors, dignities, riches, and all kinds of good, together with great tranquillity of mind; also to discover Treasures and chase away the Spirits who preside over them. It should be written upon *Virgin Parchment,* with the pen of the swallow and the blood of the screech-owl.

Editor's Note.—In the center of the Hexagram are the letters of the Name AHIH, Eheieh; in the upper and lower angles of the same, those of the Name AB, the Father; in the remaining angles those of the Name IHVH. I believe the letters outside the Hexagram in the re-entering angles to be intended for those of the first two words of the Versicle, which is taken from *Psalm cxii.* 3:—"*Wealth and Riches are in his house, and his righteousness endureth for ever.*"

Figure 20.—The Third Pentacle of Jupiter.—This defendeth and protecteth those who invoke and cause the Spirits to come. When they appear show unto them this *Pentacle* and immediately they will obey.

Editor's Note.—In the upper left hand corner is the *Magical Seal* of Jupiter with the letters of the Name IHVH. In the others are the Seal of the Intelligence of Jupiter, and the Names Adonai and IHVH. Around it is the Versicle from *Psalm cxxv.* 1:—"*A Song of degrees. They that trust in IHVH shall be as Mount Zion, which cannot be removed, but abideth for ever.*"

Figure 21.—The Fourth Pentacle of Jupiter.—It serveth to acquire riches and honor, and to possess much wealth. Its Angel is Bariel. It should be engraved upon silver in the day and hour of Jupiter when he is in the Sign Cancer.

Editor's Note.—Above the *Magical Sigil* is the Name IH, Iah. Below it are the Names of the Angels Adoniel and Bariel, the letters of the latter being arranged about a square of four compartments. Around is the Versicle from *Psalm cxii.* 3:—"*Wealth and Riches are in his house, and his righteousness endureth for ever.*"

Figure 22.—The Fifth Pentacle of Jupiter.—This hath great power. It serveth for assured visions. Jacob being armed with this *Pentacle* beheld the ladder which reached unto heaven.

Editor's Note.—The Hebrew letters within the *Pentacle* are taken from the five last words of the versicle which surrounds it, each of which contains five letters. These are, then, recombined so as to form certain Mystical Names. The versicle is taken from *Ezekiel i.* 1:—"*As I was among the captives by the river of Chebar, the heavens were opened, and I saw visions of Elohim.*" In my opinion the versicle should only consist of the five last words thereof, when the anachronism of Jacob using a *Pentacle* with a sentence from Ezekiel will not longer exist.

Figure 23.—The Sixth Pentacle of Jupiter.—It serveth for protection against all earthly dangers, by regarding it each day devoutedly, and repeating the versicle which surroundeth it. "*Thus shalt thou never perish.*"

Editor's Note.—The four Names in the Arms of the Cross are:—Seraph, Kerub, Ariel, and Tharsis; the four rulers of the Elements. The versicle is from *Psalm xxii.* 16, 17:—"*They pierced my hands and my feet, I may tell all my bones.*"

Figure 24.—The Seventh and last Pentacle of Jupiter.—It hath great power against poverty, if thou considerest it with devotion, repeating the versicle. It serveth furthermore to drive away those Spirits who guard treasures, and to discover the same.

Editor's Note.—Mystical Characters of Jupiter with the verse:—

PLATE IV.

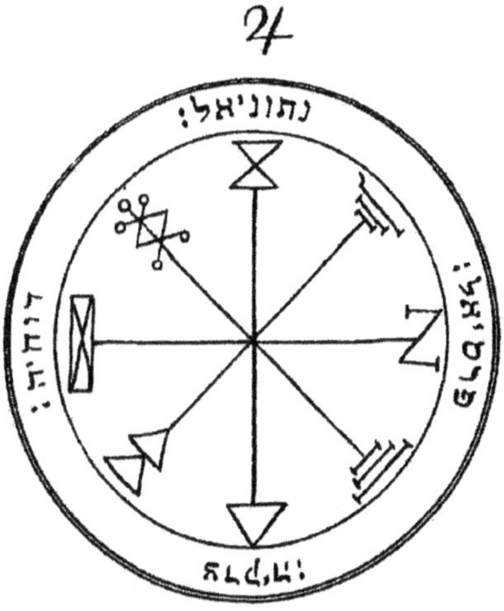

Fig. 18.

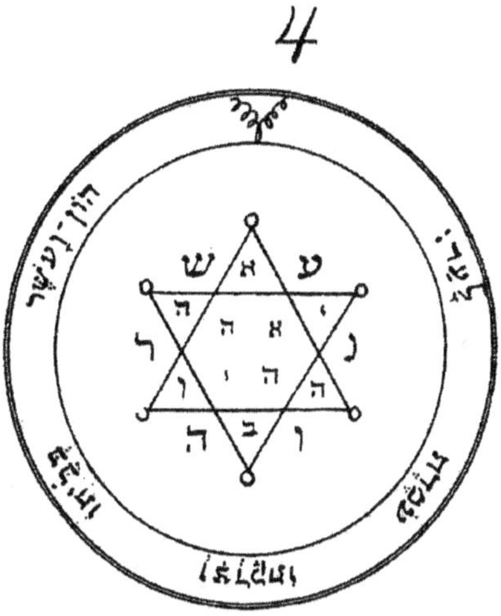

Fig. 19.

Fig. 20.

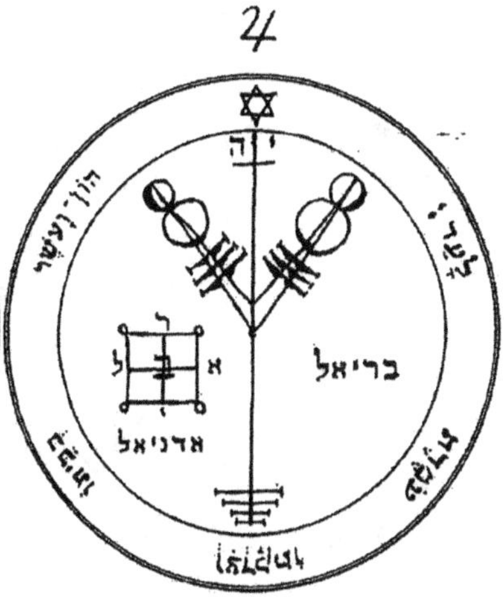

Fig. 21.

PLATE V.

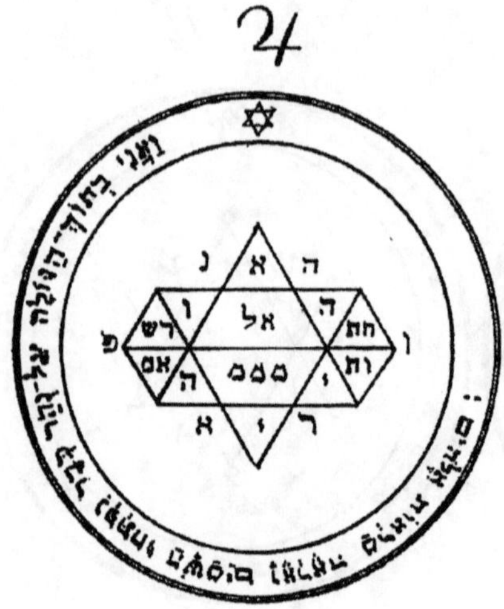

Fig. 22.

Fig. 23.

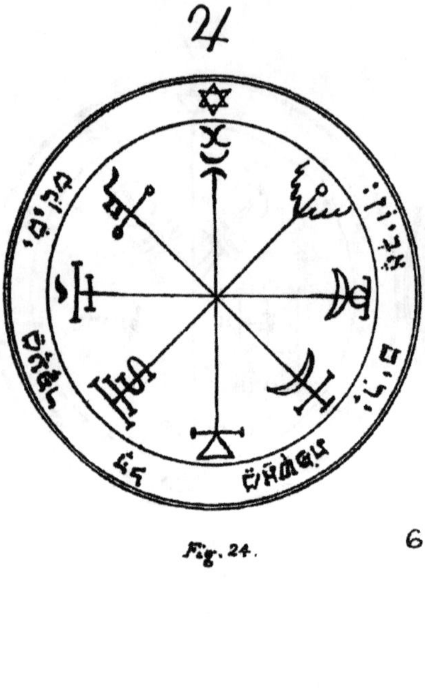

Fig. 24.

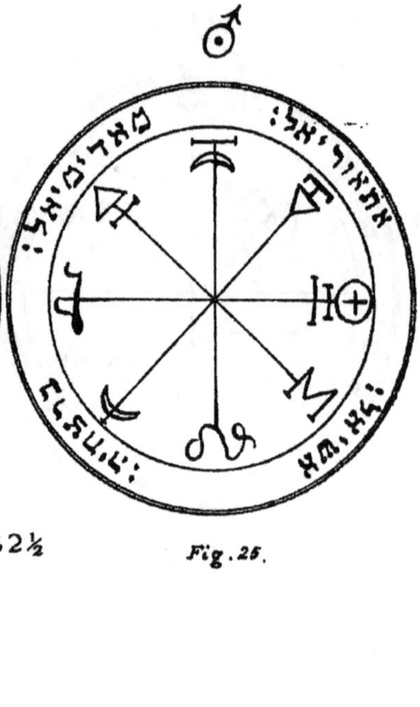

Fig. 25.

"Lifting up the poor out of the mire, and raising the needy from the dunghill, that he may set him with princes, even with the princes of his people."—Psalm cxiii. 7.

MARS.

Figure 25.—The First Pentacle of Mars.—It is proper for invoking Spirits of the Nature of Mars, especially those which are written in the *Pentacle.*

Editor's Note.—Mystical Characters of Mars, and the Names of the four Angels:—Madimiel, Bartzachiah, Eschiel, and Ithuriel written in Hebrew around the *Pentacle.*

Figure 26.—The Second Pentacle of Mars.—This *Pentacle* serveth with great success against all kinds of diseases, if it be applied unto the afflicted part.

Editor's Note.—The letter Hé, in the angles of the Hexagram. Within the same the Names IHVH, IHSHVH Yeheshuah (the mystic Hebrew Name for Joshua or Jesus, formed of the ordinary IHVH with the letter SH placed therein as emblematical of the Spirit), and Elohim. Around it is the sentence, *John i.* 4:—"In Him was life, and the life was the light of man." This *may* be adduced as an argument of the greater antiquity of the first few mystical verses of the Gospel of St. John.

Figure 27—The Third Pentacle of Mars.—It is of great value for exciting war, wrath, discord, and hostility; also for resisting enemies, and striking terror into rebellious Spirits; the Names of God the All Powerful are therein expressly marked.

Editor's Note.—The Letters of the Names Eloah and Shaddaï. In the Center is the great letter Vau, the signature of the Qabalistic Microprosopus. Around is the versicle from *Psalm lxxvii.* 13:—*"Who is so great a God as our Elohim?"*

Figure 28.—The Fourth Pentacle of Mars.—It is of great virtue and power in war, wherefore without doubt it will give thee victory.

Editor's Note.—In the Center is the great Name Agla; right and left, the letters of the Name IHVH; above and below, El. Round it is the versicle from *Psalm cx.* 5:—"*The Lord at thy right hand shall wound even Kings in the day of His Wrath.*"

Figure 29.—The Fifth Pentacle of Mars.—Write thou this *Pentacle* upon *Virgin Parchment,* because it is terrible unto the Demons, and at its sight and aspect they will obey thee, for they cannot resist its presence.

Editor's Note.—Around the figure of the Scorpion is the word HVL. The versicle is from *Psalm xci.* 13:—"*Thou shalt go upon the lion and adder, the young lion and the dragon shalt thou tread under thy feet.*"

Figure 30.—The Sixth Pentacle of Mars.—It hath so great virtue that being armed therewith, if thou art attacked by any one, thou shalt neither be injured nor wounded when thou fightest with him, and his own weapons shall turn against him.

Editor's Note.—Around the eight points of the radii of the *Pentacle* are the words "Elohim qeber, Elohim hath covered (or protected)," written in the Secret Alphabet of Malachim, or the writing of the Angels. The versicle is from *Psalm xxxvii.* 15:—"*Their sword shall enter into their own heart, and their bow shall be broken.*"

Figure 31.—The Seventh and Last Pentacle of Mars.—Write thou this upon *Virgin Parchment Paper* with the blood of a bat, in the day and hour of Mars; and uncover it within the Circle, invoking the Demons whose Names are therein written; and thou shalt immediately see hail and tempest.

Editor's Note.—In the center of the Pentacle are the Divine Names, El and Yiai, which have the same numerical value when written in Hebrew. The Letters in Hebrew, and in the Secret Alphabet called the Celestial, compose the Names of Spirits. Round the *Pentacle* is:—"*He gave them hail for rain, and flaming fire in their land. He smote their vines also, and their fig-trees.*"—*Psalm cv.* 32, 33.

Fig. 26.

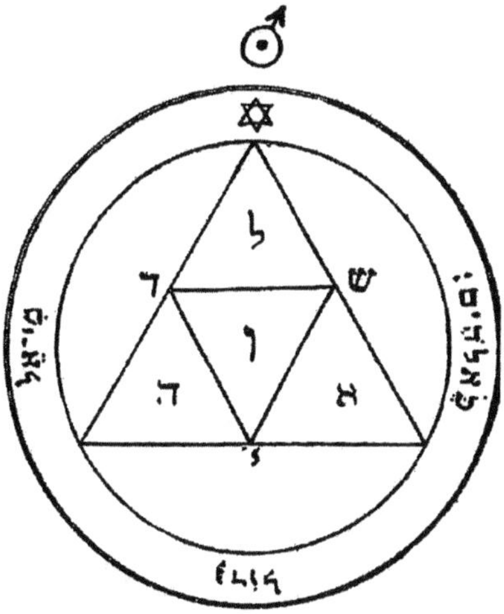

Fig. 27.

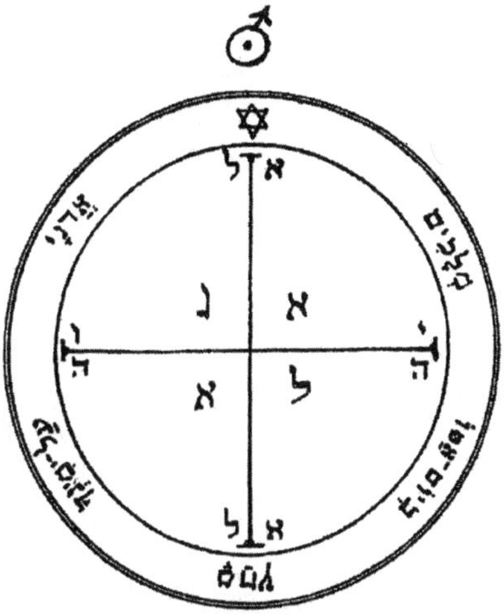

Fig. 28.

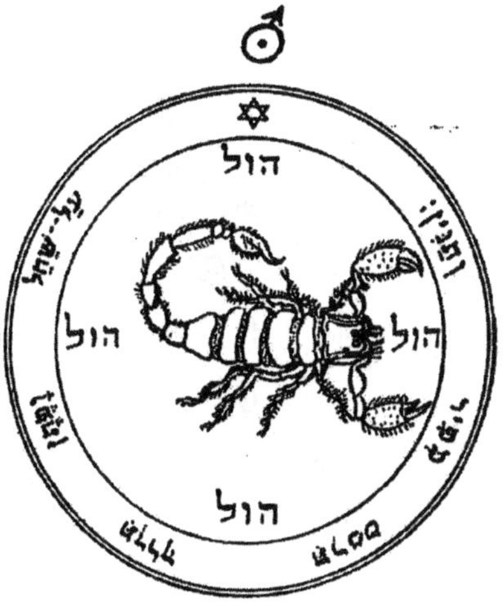

Fig. 29.

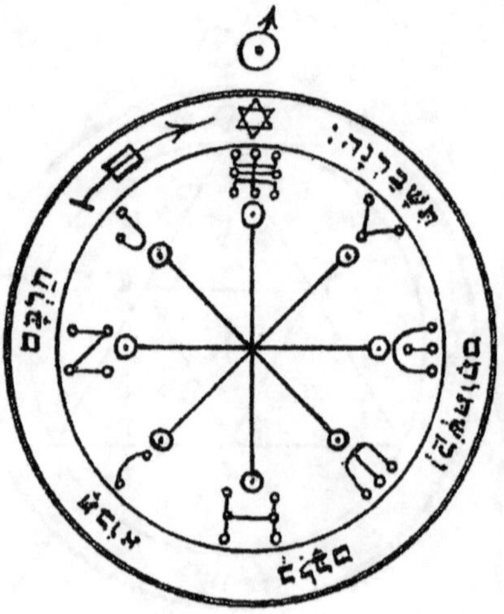

Fig. 30.

Fig. 31.

Fig. 32.

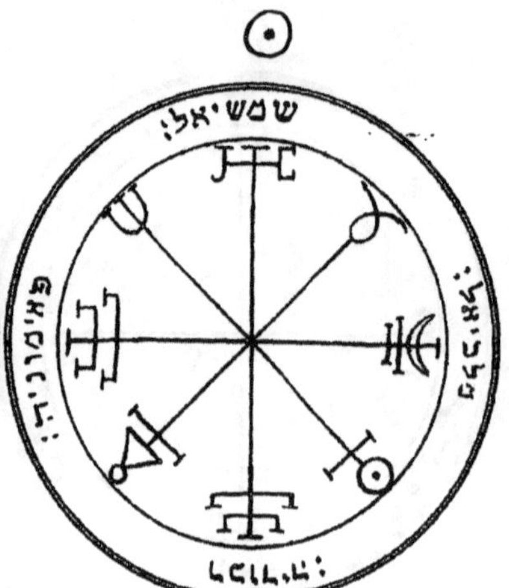

Fig. 33.

THE SUN.

Figure 32.—The First Pentacle of the Sun.—The Countenance of *Shaddaï* the Almighty, at Whose aspect all creatures obey, and the Angelic Spirits do reverence on bended knees.

Editor's Note.—This singular *Pentacle* contains the head of the great Angel Methraton or Metatron, the vice-gerent and representative of *Shaddaï*, who is called the Prince of Countenances, and the right-hand masculine Cherub of the Ark, as Sandalphon is the left and feminine. On either side is the Name "El Shaddaï." Around is written in Latin: —"*Behold His face and form by Whom all things were made, and Whom all creatures obey.*"

Figure 33.—The Second Pentacle of the Sun.—This *Pentacle*, and the preceding and following, belong to the nature of the Sun. They serve to repress the pride and arrogance of the *Solar Spirits*, which are altogether proud and arrogant by their nature.

Editor's Note.—Mystical characters of the Sun and the Names of the Angels:—Shemeshiel, Paimoniah, Rekhodiah, and Malkhiel.

Figure 34.—The Third Pentacle of the Sun.—This serveth in addition (to the effects of the two preceding) to acquire Kingdom and Empire, to inflict loss, and to acquire renown and glory, especially through the Name of God, *Tetragrammaton*, which therein is twelve times contained.

Editor's Note.—The Name IHVH, twelve times repeated; and a versicle somewhat similar to *Daniel iv.* 34:—"*My Kingdom is an everlasting Kingdom, and my dominion endureth from age to age.*"

Figure 35.—The Fourth Pentacle of the Sun.—This serveth to enable thee to see the Spirits when they appear invisible unto those who invoke them; because, when thou hast uncovered it, they will immediately appear visible.

Editor's Note.—The Names IHVH, Adonai, are written in the center in Hebrew; and round the radii in the mystical characters of the "Passing of the River." The versicle is from *Psalm xiii.* 3, 4:—"*Lighten mine eyes that I sleep not in death, lest mine enemy say, I have prevailed against him.*"

Figure 36.—The Fifth Pentacle of the Sun.—It serveth to invoke those Spirits who can transport thee from one place unto another, over a long distance and in short time.

Editor's Note.—Characters in the "*Passing of the River*" Alphabet, forming Spirit's Names. The Versicle is from *Psalm xci.* 11, 12:—"*He shall give His Angels charge over thee, to keep thee in all thy ways. They shall bear thee up in their hands.*"

Figure 37.—The Sixth Pentacle of the Sun.—It serveth excellently for the operation of invisibility, when correctly made.

Editor's Note.—In the center is the Mystical letter Yod, in the Celestial Alphabet. The three letters in the "*Passing of the River*" writing, in the Angles of the triangle, form the great Name *Shaddaï*. The wôrds in the same characters round its three sides are, in my opinion, from *Genesis* i. 1:—"*In the beginning the Elohim created, etc.*"; but the characters are sadly mangled in the MSS. The versicle is from *Psalms lxix.* 23, and *cxxxv.* 16:—"*Let their eyes be darkened that they see not; and make their loins continually to shake. They have eyes and see not.*"

Figure 38.—The Seventh and Last Pentacle of the Sun.—If any be by chance imprisoned or detained in fetters of iron, at the presence of this *Pentacle,* which should be engraved in Gold on the day and hour of the Sun, he will be immediately delivered and set at liberty.

Editor's Note.—On the Arms of the Cross are written the Names of Chasan, Angel of Air; Arel, Angel of Fire; Phorlakh, Angel of Earth; and Taliahad, Angel of Water. Between the four Arms of the Cross are written the names of the Four Rulers of the Elements; Ariel, Seraph, Tharshis, and Cherub. The versicle is from *Psalm cxvi.* 16, 17:—"*Thou hast broken my bonds in sunder. I will offer unto thee the sacrifice of thanksgiving, and will call upon the Name of IHVH.*"

VENUS.

Figure 39.—The First Pentacle of Venus.—This and those following serve to control the Spirits of Venus, and especially those herein written.

PLATE VIII.

Fig. 34.

Fig. 35.

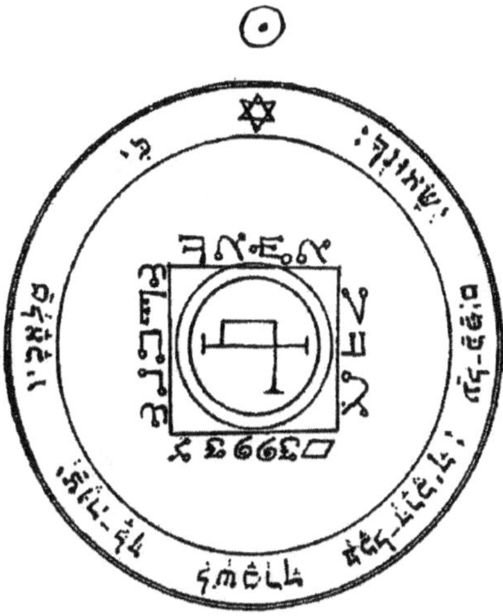

Fig. 36.

Fig. 37.

Plate IX.

Fig. 38.

Fig. 39.

Fig. 40.

Fig. 41.

Editor's Note.—Mystical Characters of Venus, and the Names of the Angels Nogahiel, Acheliah, Socodiah (or Socohiah) and Nangariel.

Figure 40.—The Second Pentacle of Venus.—These *Pentacles* are also proper for obtaining grace and honor, and for all things which belong unto *Venus,* and for accomplishing all thy desires herein.

Editor's Note.—The letters round and within the *Pentagram* form the Names of *Spirits of Venus.* The versicle is from Canticles viii. 6:—"*Place me as a signet upon thine heart, as a signet upon thine arm, for love is strong as death.*"

Figure 41.—The Third Pentacle of Venus.—This, if it be only shown unto any person, serveth to attract love. Its Angel Monachiel should be invoked in the day and hour of Venus, at one o'clock or at eight.

Editor's Note.—The following Names are written within the Figure:—IHVH, Adonai, Ruach, Achides, Ægalmiel, Monachiel, and Degaliel. The versicle is from *Genesis i.* 28:—"*And the Elohim blessed them, and the Elohim said unto them, Be ye fruitful, and multiply, and replenish the earth, and subdue it.*"

Figure 42.—The Fourth Pentacle of Venus.—It is of great power, since it compels the Spirits of Venus to obey, and to force on the instant any person thou wishest to come unto thee.

Editor's Note.—At the four Angles of the Figure are the four letters of the Name IHVH. The other letters form the Names of *Spirits of Venus, e. g.*:—Schii, Eli, Ayib, etc. The versicle is from *Genesis ii.* 23, 24:—"*This is bone of my bones, and flesh of my flesh. And they two were one flesh.*"

Figure 43.—The Fifth and Last Pentacle of Venus.—When it is only showed unto any person soever, it inciteth and exciteth wonderfully unto love.

Editor's Note.—Around the central Square are the Names Elohim, El Gebil, and two other Names which I cannot decipher, and have, therefore, given them as they stand. The characters are those of the "*Passing of the River.*" The surrounding versicle is from *Psalm xxii.* 14:—"*My heart is like wax, it is melted in the midst of my bowels.*"

MERCURY.

Figure 44.—The First Pentacle of Mercury.—It serveth to invoke the Spirits who are under the Firmament.

Editor's Note.—Letters forming the Names of the Spirits *Yekahel* and *Agiel.*

Figure 45.—The Second Pentacle of Mercury.—The Spirits herein written serve to bring to effect and to grant things which are contrary unto the order of Nature; and which are not contained under any other head. They easily give answer, but they can with difficulty be seen.

Editor's Note.—The Letters form the Names of Böel and other Spirits.

Figure 46.—The Third Pentacle of Mercury.—This and the following serve to invoke the Spirits subject unto Mercury; and especially those who are written in this *Pentacle.*

Editor's Note.—Mystical Characters of Mercury, and the Names of the Angels: Kokaviel, Gheoriah, Savaniah, and Chokmahiel.

Figure 47.—The Fourth Pentacle of Mercury.—This is further proper to acquire the understanding and Knowledge of all things created, and to seek out and penetrate into hidden things; and to command those Spirits which are called Allatori to perform embassies. They obey very readily.

Editor's Note.—In the center is the Name of God, El. The Hebrew letters inscribed about the dodecagram make the sentence, "IHVH, fix Thou the Volatile, and let there be unto the void restriction." The versicle is:—"Wisdom and virtue are in his house, and the Knowledge of all things remaineth with him for ever."

Figure 48.—The Fifth and Last Pentacle of Mercury.—This commandeth the Spirits of Mercury, and serveth to open doors in whatever way they may be closed, and nothing it may encounter can resist it.

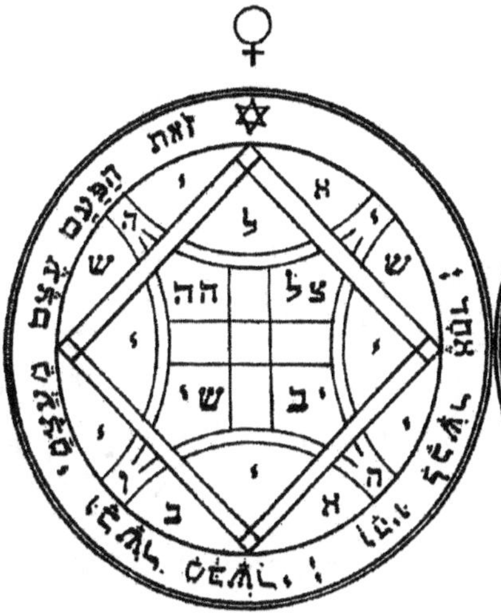

Fig. 42.

Fig. 43.

Fig. 44.

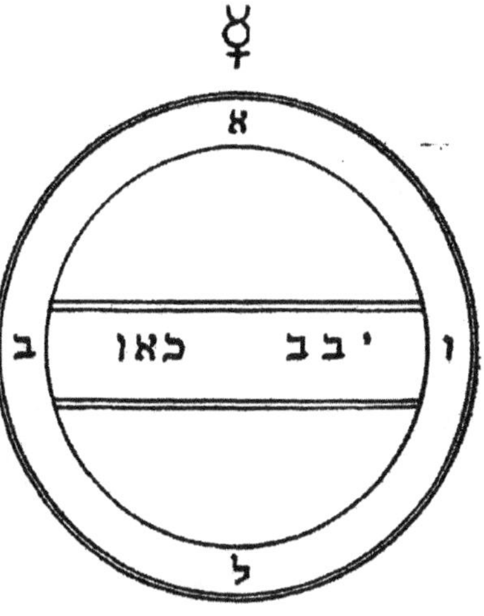

Fig. 45.

Fig. 46.

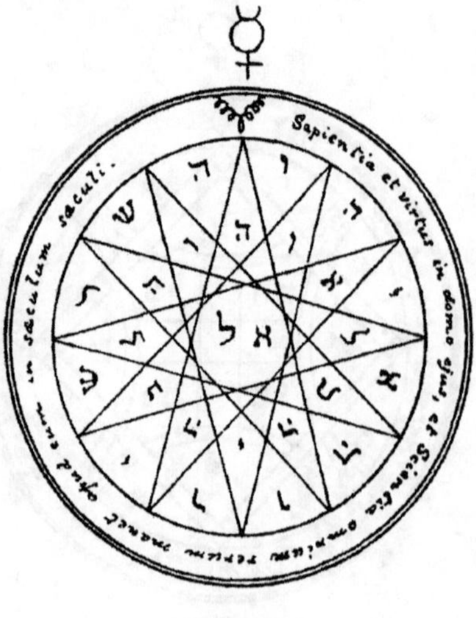

Fig. 47.

Fig. 48.

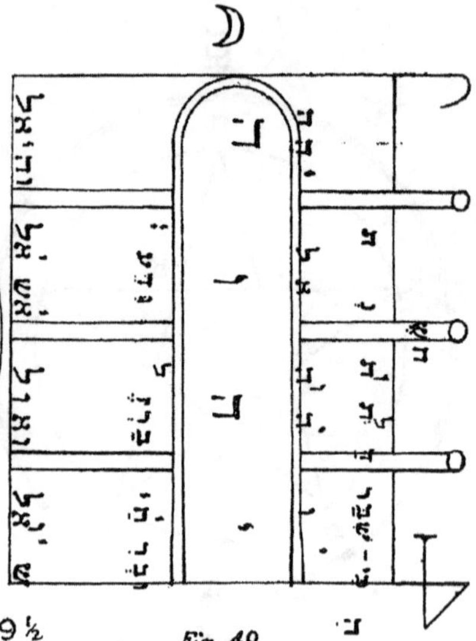

Fig. 49.

Editor's Note.—Within the Pentacle are the Names El Ab, and IHVH. The versicle is from *Psalm xxiv.* 7:—"*Lift up your heads, O ye gates, and be ye lift up ye everlasting doors, and the King of Glory shall come in.*"

THE MOON.

Figure 49.—The First Pentacle of the Moon.—This and the following serve to call forth and invoke the Spirits of the Moon; and it further serveth to open doors, in whatever way they may be fastened.

Editor's Note.—The *Pentacle* is a species of hieroglyphic representation of a door or gate. In the center is written the Name IHVH. On the right hand are the Names IHV, IHVH, AL, and IHH. On the left hand are the Names of the Angels: Schioel, Vaol, Yashiel, and Vehiel. The versicle above the Names on either side, is from *Psalm cvii.* 16:—"*He hath broken the Gates of brass, and smitten the bars of iron in sunder.*"

Figure 50.—The Second Pentacle of the Moon.—This serveth against all perils and dangers by water, and if it should chance that the Spirits of the Moon should excite and cause great rain and exceeding tempests about the Circle, in order to astonish and terrify thee; on showing unto them this *Pentacle*, it will all speedily cease.

Editor's Note.—A hand pointing to the Name *El*, and to that of the Angel Abariel. The versicle is from *Psalm lvi.* 11:—"*In Elohim have I put my trust, I will not fear, what can man do unto me?*"

Figure 51.—The Third Pentacle of the Moon.—This being duly borne with thee when upon a journey, if it be properly made, serveth against all attacks by night, and against every kind of danger and peril by Water.

Editor's Note.—The Names Aub and Vevaphel. The versicle is from *Psalm xl.* 13:—"*Be pleased O IHVH to deliver me, O IHVH make haste to help me.*"

Figure 52.—The Fourth Pentacle of the Moon.—This defendeth thee from all evil sources, and from all injury unto soul or body. Its

Angel, Sophiel, giveth the knowledge of the virtue of all herbs and stones; and unto whomsoever shall name him, he will procure the knowledge of all.

Editor's Note.—The Divine Name Eheieh Asher Eheieh, and the Names of the Angels Yahel and Sophiel. The versicle is:—"*Let them be confounded who persecute me, and let me not be confounded; let them fear, and not I.*"

Figure 53.—The Fifth Pentacle of the Moon.—It serveth to have answers in sleep. Its Angel Iachadiel serveth unto destruction and loss, as well as unto the destruction of enemies. Thou mayest also call upon him by Abdon and Dalé against all Phantoms of the night, and to summon the souls of the departed from Hades.

Editor's Note.—The Divine Names IHVH and *Elohim*, a mystical character of the Moon, and the Names of the Angels Iachadiel and Azarel. The versicle is from *Psalm lxviii.* 1:—"*Let God arise, and let His enemies be scattered; let them also who hate Him flee before Him.*"

Figure 54.—The Sixth and Last Pentacle of the Moon.—This is wonderfully good, and serveth excellently to excite and cause heavy rains, if it be engraved upon a plate of silver; and if it be placed under water, as long as it remaineth there, there will be rain. It should be engraved, drawn, or written in the day and hour of the Moon.

Editor's Note.—The Pentacle is composed of mystical characters of the Moon, surrounded by a versicle from *Genesis vii.* 11, 12:—"*All the fountains of the great deep were broken up . . . and the rain was upon the earth.*"

This is the end of the *Holy Pentacles*, in all which I have, to the best of my power, restored the Hebrew letters and mystical characters correctly. I have further given nearly every versicle in pointed Hebrew, instead of in the Latin; so that the Occult student might not be inconvenienced by having to search out the same in a Hebrew Bible. The restoration of the Hebrew letters in the body of the *Pentacles* has been a work of immense difficulty, and has extended over several years.—Dr. de Laurence.

PLATE XII.

Fig. 50.

Fig. 51

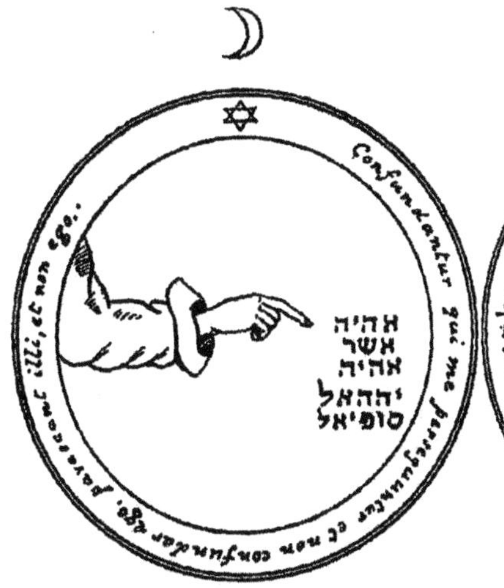

Fig. 52.

Fig. 53.

PREFATORY NOTE TO BOOK TWO.

THIS Work of SOLOMON is divided into TWO BOOKS. In the first thou mayest see and know how to avoid errors in Experiments, Operations, and in the Spirits themselves. In the second thou art taught in what manner Magical Arts may be reduced to the proposed object and end.

It is for this reason that thou shouldst take great heed and care that this Key of Secrets* fall not into the hands of the foolish, the stupid, and the ignorant. For he who is the possessor hereof, and who availeth himself hereof according to the ordinances herein contained, will not only be able to reduce the Magical Arts herein unto their proposed end, but will, even if he findeth certain errors herein, be able to correct them.

Any Art or Operation of this kind will not be able to attain its end, unless the Master of the Art, or Exorcist, shall have this Work completely in his power, that is to say, unless he thoroughly understand it, for without this he will never attain the effect of any operation.

For this reason I earnestly pray and conjure the person into whose hands this Key of Secrets may fall, neither to communicate it, nor to make any one a partaker in this knowledge, if he be not faithful, nor capable of keeping a secret, nor expert in the Arts. And I most humbly entreat the possessor of this, by the Ineffable Name of God in Four Letters, YOD, HE, VAU, HE, and by the Name ADONAI, and by all the other Most High and Holy Names of God, that he values this work as dearly as his own soul, and that he makes no foolish or ignorant man a partaker therein.

* This Prefatory Note is only found in 3981 *Harleian* MSS., 3091 *Sloane* MSS., and 288 King's MSS.

The Key Of Solomon.

The Beginning Of Book Two.

BOOK TWO.

CHAPTER I.

At What Hour After the Preparation of All Things Necessary, We Should Bring the Exercise of the Art to Perfection.

The Days and Hours have already been treated of, in general, in the First Book. It is now necessary to notice in particular at what hour accomplishment and perfection should be given to the Arts, all things necessary having been previously prepared.

Should it then happen that thou hast undertaken any secret operation for conversing with or conjuring Spirits, in which the day and the hour are not marked, thou shalt put it in execution on the days and hours of Mercury, at the sixteenth or twenty-third hour, but it will be still better at the eighth, which is the third of the same night, which is called and means before the morning, for then thou shalt be able to put in practice all the Arts and Operations which should be performed, according as it shall please thee by day or by night, provided that they have been prepared at the hours suitable to them, as hath been already said. But when neither hour nor time of operation or invocation is specified, it is then much better to perform these experiments at night, seeing that it is more easy to the Spirits to appear in the peaceful silence of night than during the day. And thou shouldst inviolably observe, that wishing to invoke the Spirits, either by day or by night, it is necessary that it should be done in a place hidden, removed, secret, convenient, and proper for such Art, where no man frequenteth or inhabiteth, as we shall relate more fully in its place.

If then thou shouldst operate touching anything which hath been stolen, in whatever way it be performed and whatever way it may have been prepared, it is necessary to practice it on the days and hours of the Moon, being if possible in her increase, and from the first unto the eighth hour of the day.

But if it be by night, then it should be at the fifth or at the third hour; but it is better by day than by the night, for the light justifieth them, and maketh them much more fit for publication. But if the Operations be regarding Invisibility, they should be put in practice at the first, second, and third hours of Mars by day. But if by night, until the third hour. If they be Operations of seeking love, grace, or favor, they should be performed until the eighth hour of the same day, commencing with the first hour of the Sun; and from the first hour of Venus unto the first hour of the same day of Venus.

As for Operations of destruction and desolation, we should practice and put them into execution on the day of Saturn at the first hour, or rather at the eighth or fifteenth of the day; and from the first until the eighth hour of the night.

Experiments of games, raillery, deceit, illusion, and invisibility, ought to be done at the first hour of Venus, and at the eighth hour of the day; but by night at the third and at the seventh.

At all times of practicing and putting into execution Magical Arts, the Moon should be increasing in light, and in an equal number of degrees with the Sun; and it is much better from the first quarter to the Opposition, and the Moon should be in a fiery Sign, and notably in that of the Ram or of the Lion.

Therefore, to execute these Experiments in any manner whatsoever, it should be done when the Moon is clear, and when she is increasing in light.

In order to put in execution those of Invisibility after everything is properly prepared, the Moon should be in the Sign of the Fishes, in the hours proper and fitting, and she should be increasing in light.

For experiments of seeking love and favor, in whatever way it may be desired, they will succeed, provided that they have been prepared at the proper hours, and that the Moon be increasing in light and in the Sign of the Twins.

So exact a preparation of days and hours is not necessary for those who are Adepts in the Art, but it is extremely necessary for apprentices and beginners, seeing that those who have been little or not at all instructed herein, and who only begin to apply themselves to this Art, do not have as much faith in the experiments as those who are adepts therein, and who have practiced them. But as regards beginners, they should always have the days and hours well disposed and appropriate unto the Art. And the Wise should only observe the precepts of the Art which are necessary, and in observing the other solemnities necessary they will operate with a perfect assurance.

It is, nevertheless, necessary to take care that when thou shalt have prepared any experiment thyself for the days and hours ordained, that it should be performed in clear, serene, mild, and pleasant weather, without any great tempest or agitation of the air, which should not be troubled by winds. For when thou shalt have conjured any Spirits in any art or experiment, they will not come when the Air is troubled or agitated by winds, seeing that Spirits have neither flesh nor bones, and are created of different substances.

Some are created from Water.

Others from Wind, unto which they are like.

Some from Earth.

Some from Clouds.

Others from Solar Vapors.

Others from the keenness and strength of Fire; and when they are invoked or summoned, they come always with great noise, and with the terrible nature of fire.

When the Spirits which are created of Water are invoked, they come with great rains, thunder, hail, lightning, thunder-bolts, and the like.

When the Spirits which are created of Clouds are invoked, they come with great deformity, in a horrible form, to strike fear into the Invocator, and with an exceeding great noise.

Others* which are formed from wind appear like thereunto and with exceeding swift motion, and whensoever those which are created from Beauty† appear, they will show themselves in a fair and agreeable form; moreover, whensoever thou shalt call the Spirits created from Air, they will come with a kind of gentle breeze.

When the Spirits which are created from the Vapors of the Sun are invoked, they come under a very beautiful and excellent form, but filled with pride, vanity, and conceit. They are clever, whence it comes that these last are all specified by SOLOMON in his book of ornament, or of beauty. They show great ostentation and vainglory in their dress, and they rejoice in many ornaments; the boast of possessing mundane beauty, and all sorts of ornaments and decorations. Thou shalt only invoke them in serene, mild, and pleasant weather.

The Spirits which are created of Fire reside in the east, those created of Wind in the south.

Note then that it will be much better to perform the experiments or operations in the direction of the East, putting everything necessary in practice towards that point.

But for all other operations or extraordinary experiments, and for those of love, they will be much more efficacious directed towards the north.

Take heed further, that every time that thou performest any experiment, to reduce it unto perfection with the requisite solemnities, thou shalt recommence the former experiment if interrupted therein, without the preparation of hours or other solemnities.

If by chance it should happen that having performed an experiment with due observance of days, hours, and requisite solemnities, thou shalt find it unsuccessful, it must be in some manner false, ill-arranged and defective, and thou must assuredly have failed in some matter; for if thou doest ill in one single point, these experiments or these Arts will not be verified.

Thus upon this Chapter dependeth this whole *Key of Arts, Experiments, and Operations*, and although every solemnity be rightly observed, no experiment will be verified, unless thou canst penetrate the meaning of this Chapter.

* This paragraph is only found in 10862 Add. MSS.

† The Name of the Sixth Qabalistical Sephira or Emanation from the Deity, which is called Tiphereth, or Beauty.

BOOK TWO.

CHAPTER II.

In What Manner the Master of the Art Should Keep, Rule, and Govern Himself.

He who wisheth to apply himself unto so great and so difficult a Science should have his mind free from all business, and from all extraneous ideas of whatever nature they may be.

He should then thoroughly examine the Art or Operation which he should undertake, and write it regularly out on paper, particularly set aside for that purpose, with the appropriate conjurations and exorcisms. If there be anything to mark or write down, it should be performed in the manner specified regarding the paper, ink, and pen. He should also observe at what day and at what hour this Experiment should be undertaken, and what things are necessary to prepare for it, what should be added, and what can be dispensed with.

The which matters being prepared, it is necessary for thee to search out and arrange some fitting place wherein the Magical Art and its Experiments can be put in practice. All these things being thus arranged and disposed, let the Master of the Art go into a proper and fitting place, or into his Cabinet or Secret Chamber if it be convenient for the purpose, and he can there dispose and set in order the whole operation; or he can use any other convenient secret place for the purpose, provided that no one knoweth where it is, and that no man can see him when there.

After this he must strip himself entirely naked, and let him have a bath ready prepared, wherein is water exorcised, after the manner which we shall describe, so that he may bathe and purify himself therein from the crown of his head unto the sole of his foot, saying:—

O Lord Adonai, Who hast formed me Thine unworthy servant in Thine Image and resemblance of vile and of abject earth; deign to bless and to sanctify this Water, so that it may be for the health and purification of my soul, and of my body, so that no foolishness or deceitfulness may therein in any way have place.

O Most Powerful and Ineffable God, Who madest Thy people pass dryshod through the *Red Sea* when they came up out of the Land of Egypt, grant unto me grace that I may be purified and regenerated from all my past sins by this Water, that so no uncleanness may appear upon me in Thy Presence.

After this thou shalt entirely immerse thyself in the Water, and thou shalt dry thyself with a towel of clean white linen, and then thou shalt put upon thy flesh the garments of pure white linen whereof we shall speak hereafter.

Hereafter, for three days at least, thou shalt abstain from all idle, vain, and impure reasonings, and from every kind of impurity and sin, as will be shown in the Chapter of fast and of vigil. Each day shalt thou recite the following prayer, at least once in the morning, twice about noon, thrice in the afternoon, four times in the evening, and five times before lying down to sleep; this shalt thou do on the three ensuing days:—

THE PRAYER.

HERACHIO, ASAC, ASACRO, BEDRIMULAEL, TILATH, ARABONAS, IERAHLEM, IDEODOC, ARCHARZEL, ZOPHIEL, BLAUTEL, BARACATA, EDONIEL, ELOHIM, EMAGRO, ABRAGATEH, SAMOEL, GEBURAHEL, CADATO, ERA, ELOHI, ACHSAH, EBMISHA, IMACHEDEL, DANIEL, DAMA, ELAMOS, IZACHEL, BAEL, SEGON, GEMON, DEMAS.

O Lord God, Who art seated upon the Heavens, and Who regardest the Abysses beneath, grant unto me Thy Grace I beseech Thee, so that what I conceive in my mind I may accomplish in my work, through Thee, O God, the Sovereign Ruler of all, Who livest and reignest unto the Ages of the Ages. Amen.

These three days having passed, thou must have all things in readiness, as hath been said, and after this a day appointed and set apart. It will be necessary for thee to wait for the hour in which thou shouldst commence the Operation; but when once it shall be commenced at this hour, thou shalt be able to continue it unto the end, seeing that it deriveth its force and virtue from its beginning, which extendeth to and spreadeth over the succeeding hours, so that the Master of the Art will be enabled to complete his work so as to arrive at the desired result.

BOOK TWO.

CHAPTER III.

HOW THE COMPANIONS OR DISCIPLES OF THE MASTER OF THE ART OUGHT TO REGULATE AND GOVERN THEMSELVES.

WHEN the Master of the Art wisheth to put in practice any Operation or Experiment, especially one of importance, he should first consider of what Companions he should avail himself. This is the reason why in every Operation whose Experience should be carried out in the Circle, it is well to have three Companions. And if he cannot have Companions, he should at least have with him a faithful and attached dog. But if it be absolutely necessary for him to have Companions, these Companions should be obligated and bound by oath to do all that the Master shall order or prescribe them, and they should study, observe, and carefully retain, and be attentive unto all which they shall hear. For those who shall act otherwise shall suffer and endure many pains and labors, and run into many dangers, which the Spirits will cause and procure for them, and for this cause sometimes they shall even die.

The Disciples then, being well and thoroughly instructed, and fortified with a wise and understanding heart, the Master shall take exorcised Water, and he shall enter with his Disciples into a secret place purified and clean, where he must strip them entirely naked; after this, let him pour exorcised water upon their heads, which he should cause to flow from the crown of their head unto the sole of their foot, so as to bathe them entirely therewith; and while bathing them thus, he should say:—

Be ye regenerate, cleansed, and purified, in the Name of the Ineffable, Great, and Eternal God, from all your iniquities, and may the virtue of the Most High descend upon you and abide with you always, so that ye may have the power and strength to accomplish the desires of your heart. Amen.

After this let the Disciples robe themselves as the Master hath done, and fast like him for three days, repeating the same prayer; let them act like him, and in the work let them implicitly follow and obey him in all things.

But if the Master of the Art wisheth to have a dog for his Companion, he must bathe him thoroughly with the exorcised water in the same manner as the Disciples, and let him perfume him with the odors and incense of Art, and let him repeat the following Conjuration over him:—

I conjure thee, O thou Creature, being a Dog, by Him Who hath created thee, I bathe and I perfume thee in the Name of the Most High, Most Powerful, and Eternal God, so that thou mayest be my true Companion in this operation, and that thou mayest be also my faithful friend in whatsoever Operation I may hereafter perform.

But if he wisheth to have for his companion a little boy or girl, which will be still better, he must ordain them as he hath ordained the dog; and he must pare and cut the nails of their hands and of their feet, saying:—

I conjure thee, O thou Creature, being a young girl (or boy), by the Most High God, the Father of all Creatures, by the Father ADONAI ELOHIM, and by the Father ELION, that thou shalt have neither will nor power to hide from me anything, nor yet to keep back from me the truth in all which I shall demand of thee, and that thou be obedient and faithful unto me. Amen.

Let him purify, cleanse, and wash this young child anew, with the Water of Art, saying:—

Be thou regenerate, cleansed, and purified, so that the Spirits may neither harm thee nor abide in thee. Amen.

Then perfume the child with odours as above.

When the companions shall be thus ordained and disposed, the Master shalt be able to operate in surety together with them, every time that it shall please him; and he shall perform his operation happily, and shall attain his end.

But for the safety both of soul and of body, the Master and the Companions should have the Pentacles before their breasts, consecrated, and covered with a silken veil, and perfumed with the proper fumigations. By the which being assured and encouraged, they may enter into the matter without fear or terror, and they shall be exempt and free from all perils and dangers, provided that they obey the commands of the Master and do all that he ordain them. If they shall act thus, all things shall go according unto their desires.

All being thus arranged, the Master should take heed that His Disciples are perfectly instructed in those things which they have to perform.

These Companions or Disciples should be three in number, without including the Master. They may also be of the number of five, of seven, or of nine; but so that they ever implicitly obey the orders of their Master; for thus only shall all things come to a successful issue.

BOOK TWO.

CHAPTER IV.

Concerning the Fasting, Care, and Things to Be Observed.

When the Master of the Art shall wish to perform his operations, having previously arranged all things which it is necessary to observe and practise; from the first day of the Experiment, it is absolutely necessary to ordain and to prescribe care and observation, to abstain from all things unlawful, and from every kind of impiety, impurity, wickedness, or immodesty, as well of body as of soul; as, for example, eating and drinking superabundantly, and all sorts of vain words, buffooneries, slanders, calumnies, and other useless discourse; but instead to do good deeds, speak honestly, keep a strict decency in all things, never lose sight of modesty in walking, in conversation, in eating and drinking, and in all things; the which should be principally done and observed for nine days, before the commencement of the Operation. The Disciples should do the same, and should equally put in practice all things necessary to be observed, if they wish to make use of all these operations and experiments.

But before the commencement of the work, it is absolutely necessary that the Master with his Disciples repeat the following Conjuration once in the morning, and twice in the evening:—

THE CONJURATION.

O Lord God Almighty, be propitious unto me a miserable sinner, for I am not worthy to raise mine eyes unto heaven, because of the iniquity of my sins and the multitude of my faults. O pitying and merciful Father, who wouldest not the death of a sinner but rather that he should turn from his wickedness and live, O God have mercy upon me and pardon all my sins; for I unworthy entreat Thee, O Father of all Creatures, Thou Who art full of mercy and of compassion, by Thy great goodness, that Thou deign to grant unto me power to see and know these Spirits which I desire to behold and to invoke to appear before me and to accomplish my will. Through Thee Who art Conqueror, and Who art Blessed unto the Ages of the Ages. Amen.

O Lord God the Father Eternal, Who art seated upon the Kerubim and the Seraphim, Who lookest upon Earth and upon Sea; unto Thee do I raise my hands and implore thine aid alone, Thou Who alone art the accomplishment of good works, Thou Who givest rest unto those who labour, Who humblest the proud, Who art the Author of Life and the Destroyer of Death; Thou art our rest, Thou art the Protector of those who invoke Thee; protect, guard, and defend me in this matter, and in this enterprise which I propose to carry out, O Thou Who livest, reignest, and abidest unto the Eternal Ages. Amen.

During the three last days before the commencement of this action, thou shalt content thyself with only eating fasting diet, and that only once in the day; and it will be better still if thou only partakest of bread and water. Thou shalt also abstain from every impure thing; reciting the prayer above written. And on the last day, when thou shalt wish to commence the Operation, thou shalt remain all day without eating, and later on thou shalt go into a secret place, where thou shalt confess all thy sins unto God with a contrite heart. The Disciples also, together with the Master, shall recite the same Confession with a low but distinct voice, as hath been already said in the *First Book*.

This having been done thrice with a devout, pure, and contrite heart, in a place withdrawn from men, cleansed, and pure, where thou canst not be seen, taking the water and the hyssop, thou shalt say:—

Purify me, O Lord, with hyssop, and I shall be pure; wash me and I shall be whiter than snow.

After this, bathe thyself with the exorcised water, and clothe thyself again with the consecrated garment which thou hast taken off; cense thyself, and surround thyself with odours, as will be told farther on, when we speak of perfumes and suffumigations.

The which being done, thou shalt go unto the ordained place with thy Companions, and all things being prepared, thou shalt make the Circle, as hath been already said, with all other necessary ceremonies; then shalt thou commence to invoke the Spirits by the Exorcisms; thou shalt also repeat anew the foregoing Confession as hath been already said in the First Book. After which, in sign of amendment and of repentance, each shall mutually kiss the other.

Mark well, that up to this point, the Disciples should do the same things as the Master.

Let the Master now give his commands unto his Disciples, and pursue the course of the Experiment, and work with all diligence to bring it unto perfection.

BOOK TWO.

CHAPTER V.

Concerning the Baths, and How They Are to Be Arranged.

The Bath is necessary for all *Magical and Necromantic Arts;* wherefore, if thou wishest to perform any experiment or operation, having arranged all things necessary thereunto according to the proper days and hours, thou shalt go unto a river or running stream, or thou shalt have warm water ready in some large vessel or tub in thy secret cabinet, and while disrobing thyself of thy raiment thou shalt repeat the following Psalms:—Psalms xiv. or liii.; xxvii.; liv.; lxxxi.; cv.

And when the Master shall be entirely disrobed let him enter into the water or into the Bath, and let him say:—

THE EXORCISM OF THE WATER.

I exorcise Thee, O Creature of Water, by Him Who hath created thee and gathered thee together into one place so that the dry land appeared, that thou uncover all the deceits of the Enemy, and that thou cast out from thee all the impurities and uncleannesses of the Spirits of the World of Phantasm, so they may harm me not, through the virtue of God almighty who liveth and reigneth unto the Ages of the Ages. Amen.

Then shalt thou begin to wash thyself thoroughly in the Bath, saying:—

Mertalia, Musalia, Dophalia, Onemalia, Zitanseia, Goldaphaira, Dedulsaira, Ghevialaira, Gheminaira, Gegropheira, Cedahi, Gilthar, Godieb, Ezoiil, Musil, Grassil, Tamen, Pueri, Godu, Huznoth, Astachoth, Tzabaoth, Adonai, Agla, On, El, Tetragrammaton, Shema, Aresion, Anaphaxeton, Segilaton, Primeumaton.

All the which Names thou shalt repeat twice or thrice, until thou art completely washed and clean, and when thou art perfectly pure thou shalt quit the Bath, and sprinkle thyself with exorcised water, in the manner described later on, and thou shalt say:—

Purge me, O Lord, with hyssop, and I shall be clean; wash me, and I shall be whiter than snow.

Whilst again clothing thyself, thou shalt recite the following Psalms: Psalms cii.; li.; iv.; xxx.; cxix., *Mem.*, v. 97.; cxiv.; cxxvi., cxxxix.

After which thou shalt recite the following prayer:—

PRAYER.

El Strong and Wonderful, I bless Thee, I adore Thee, I glorify Thee, I invoke Thee, I render Thee thanks from this Bath, so that this

Water may be able to cast from me all impurity and concupiscence of heart, through Thee, O Holy ADONAI; and may I accomplish all things through Thee Who livest and reignest unto the Ages of the Ages. Amen.

After this take the Salt and bless it in this manner:—

THE BENEDICTION OF THE SALT.

The Blessing of the Father Almighty be upon this Creature of Salt, and let all malignity and hindrance be cast forth hencefrom, and let all good enter herein, for without Thee man cannot live, wherefore I bless thee and invoke thee, that thou mayest aid me.

Then thou shalt recite over the Salt, Psalm ciii.

Then taking the grains of the exorcised Salt thou shalt cast them into the aforesaid Bath; and thou shalt again disrobe thyself, pronouncing the following words:—

IMANEL, ARNAMON, IMATO, MEMEON, RECTACON, MUOBOII, PALTELLON, DECAION, YAMENTON, YARON, TATONON, VAPHORON, GARDON, EXISTON, ZAGVERON, MOMERTON, ZARMESITON, TILEION, TIXMION.

After this thou shalt enter a second time into the Bath and recite Psalms civ. and lxxxi.

Then thou shalt quit the Bath and clothe thyself as before in linen garments clean and white, and over them thou shalt put the garments, of which we shall speak in the proper Chapter, and thus clothed thou shalt go to finish thy work.

The Disciples should wash themselves in like manner, and with like solemnities.

BOOK TWO.

CHAPTER VI.

Of the Garments and Shoes of the Art.

The exterior habiliments which the Master of the Art should wear ought to be of linen, as well as those which he weareth beneath them; and if he hath the means they should be of Silk. If they be of linen the thread of which they are made should have been spun by a young maiden.

The characters shown in *Figure* 55 should be embroidered on the breast with the needle of Art in red silk.

The shoes should also be White, upon the which the characters in *Figure* 56 should be traced in the same way.

The shoes or boots should be made of white leather, on the which should be marked the Signs and Characters of Art. These shoes should be made during the days of fast and abstinence, namely, during the nine days set apart before the beginning of the Operation, during which the necessary instruments also should be prepared, polished, brightened, and cleaned.

Besides this, the Master of the Art should have a *Crown* made of *Virgin Parchment* paper, upon the which should be written these four Names:—Yod, He, Vau, He, in front; Adonai behind; El on the right; and Elohim on the left. (*See Figure* 57.) These names should be written with the ink and pen of the Art, whereof we shall speak in the proper Chapter. The Disciples should also each have a Crown of Virgin paper whereon these Divine symbols should be marked in scarlet. (*See Figure* 58.)

Take heed also that in clothing thyself with these aforesaid habiliments, that thou recite these Psalms:—Psalms xv.; cxxxi.; cxxxvii.; cxvii.; lxvii.; lxviii.; and cxxvii.

After this perfume the *Vestments* by burning *Temple Incense,* and sprinkle them with the water and hyssop of the Art.

But when the Master and His Disciples shall commence to robe themselves after the first Psalm, and before continuing with the others, he should pronounce these words:—

Amor, Amator, Amides, Ideodaniach, Pamor, Plaior, Anitor; through the merits of these holy Angels will I robe and indue myself with the Vestments of Power, through which may I conduct unto the desired end those things which I ardently wish, through Thee, O Most Holy Adonai, Whose Kingdom and Empire endureth for ever. Amen.

Take notice that if the linen garments were vestments of the Levites or of the Priests, and had been used for holy things, that they would be all the better.

BOOK TWO.

CHAPTER VII.

Of Places Wherein We May Conveniently Execute the Experiments and Operations of the Art.

The places best fitted for exercising and accomplishing Magical Arts and Operations are those which are concealed, removed, and separated from the habitations of men. Wherefore desolate and uninhabited regions are most appropriate, such as the borders of lakes, forests, dark and obscure places, old and deserted houses, whither rarely and scarce ever men do come, mountains, caves, caverns, grottos, gardens, orchards; but best of all are cross-roads, and where four roads meet, during the depth and silence of night. But if thou canst not conveniently go unto any of these places, thy house, and even thine own chamber, or, indeed, any place, provided it hath been purified and consecrated with the necessary ceremonies, will be found fit and convenient for the convocation and assembling of the Spirits.

These Arts or Operations should be carried out at the prescribed time, but if there be no time specially appointed it will be always better to perform them at night, which is the most fit and proper time for the Operations of Necromancy; this is also a symbol that it is just and right to hide them from the sight of the foolish, the ignorant, and the profane.

But when thou shalt have selected a place fitting, thou mayest perform thine experiments by day or by night. It should be spacious, clear, and bounded on all sides by hedges, shrubs, trees, or walls. Thou shalt thyself cleanse it thoroughly and render it neat and pure, and while doing this thou shalt recite Psalms ii.; lxvii.; and liv.

After this thou shalt perfume it with the odours and suffumigations of the Art, and shalt sprinkle it with the water and the hyssop; and after this thou mayest in this place make all the necessary preparations for an operation.

But when, later on, thou shalt go unto this place, to complete and accomplish the operation, thou shalt repeat on the way thither the following Prayer in a low and distinct voice:—

THE PRAYER.

Zazaii, Zamaii, Puidamon Most Powerful, Sedon Most Strong, El, Yod He Vau He, Iah, Agla, assist me an unworthy sinner who have had the boldness to pronounce these Holy Names which no man should name and invoke save in very great danger. Therefore have I recourse

unto these Most Holy Names, being in great peril both of soul and of body. Pardon me if I have sinned in any manner, for I trust in Thy protection alone, especially on this journey.

Let the Master as he goeth sprinkle the path with the water and hyssop of the Art, while each of his Disciples shall repeat in a low voice the Prayer which we have enjoined for the days of fasting and preparation.

Furthermore, let the Master appoint his Disciples to carry the things necessary for the Art.

The first shall bear the Censer, the Fire, and the Incense.

The Second; the Book, the Paper, the Pens, the Ink, and the various Perfumes.

The Third; the Knife, and the Sickle.

The Master; the Staff, and the Wand.

But if there be more Disciples present, the Master shall distribute the things for each to carry, according to their number.

When they shall have arrived at the place, and all things being disposed in their proper order, the Master shall take the Knife or other convenient consecrated Magical implement of Steel, wherewith to form the Circle of Art which he intends to construct. This being done, he must perfume it, and sprinkle it with water; and having warned and exhorted his Disciples, he shall work thus:—

First let him have a Trumpet made of new wood, on the one side of which shall be written in Hebrew with the pen and ink of the Art these Names of God, ELOHIM GIBOR, ELOHIM TZABAOTH (*see Figure* 59); and on the other side these characters (*see Figure* 60).

Having entered into the Circle to perform the Experiment, he should sound his Trumpet towards the four quarters of the Universe, first towards the East, then towards the South, then towards the West, and lastly towards the North. Then let him say:—

Hear ye, and be ye ready, in whatever part of the Universe ye may be, to obey the Voice of God the Mighty One, and the Names of the Creator. We let you know by this signal and sound that ye will be convoked hither, wherefore hold ye yourselves in readiness to obey our commands.

This being done let the Master complete his work, renew the Circle, and make the incensements and fumigations.

BOOK TWO.

CHAPTER VIII.

Of the Knife, Sword, Sickle, Poniard, Dagger, Lance, Wand, Staff, and Other Instruments of Magical Art.

In order to properly carry out the greatest and most important Operations of the Art, various Instruments are necessary, as a Knife with a white hilt, another with a black hilt, a short Lance, wherewith to trace Circles, Characters, and other things.

The Knife with the white hilt (*see Figure* 61) should be made in the day and hour of Mercury, when Mars is in the Sign of the Ram or of the Scorpion. It should be dipped in the blood of a gosling and in the juice of the pimpernel, the Moon being at her full or increasing in light. Dip therein also the white hilt, upon the which thou shalt have engraved the Characters shown. Afterwards perfume it with the perfumes of the Art.

With this Knife thou mayest perform all the necessary Operations of the Art, except the Circles. But if it seemeth unto thee too troublesome to make a similar Knife, have one made in the same fashion; and thou shalt place it thrice in the fire until it becometh red-hot, and each time thou shalt immerse it in the aforesaid blood and juice, fasten thereunto the white hilt having engraved thereon the aforesaid characters, and upon the hilt thou shalt write with the pen of Art, commencing from the point and going towards the hilt, these Names Agla, On, as shown in *Figure* 61. Afterwards thou shalt perfume and sprinkle it, and shalt wrap it in a piece of silken cloth.

But as for the Knife with the black hilt (*see Figure* 62) for making the Circle, wherewith to strike terror and fear into the Spirits, it should be made in the same manner, except that it should be done in the day and hour of Saturn, and dipped in the blood of a black cat and in the juice of hemlock, the Characters and Names shown in *Figure* 62 being written thereon, from the point towards the hilt. Which being completed, thou shalt wrap it in a black silk cloth.

The Scimitar (*Figure* 63), and the Sickle (*Figure* 64), are made in the same way, as also the Dagger (*Figure* 65), the Poniard (*Figure* 66), and the short Lance (*Figure* 67), in the day and hour of Mercury, and they should be dipped in the blood of a magpie and the juice of the herb Mercury. Thou must make for them handles of white boxwood cut at a single stroke from the tree, at the rising of the Sun, with a new knife, or with any other convenient instrument. The characters shown should

PLATE XIII.

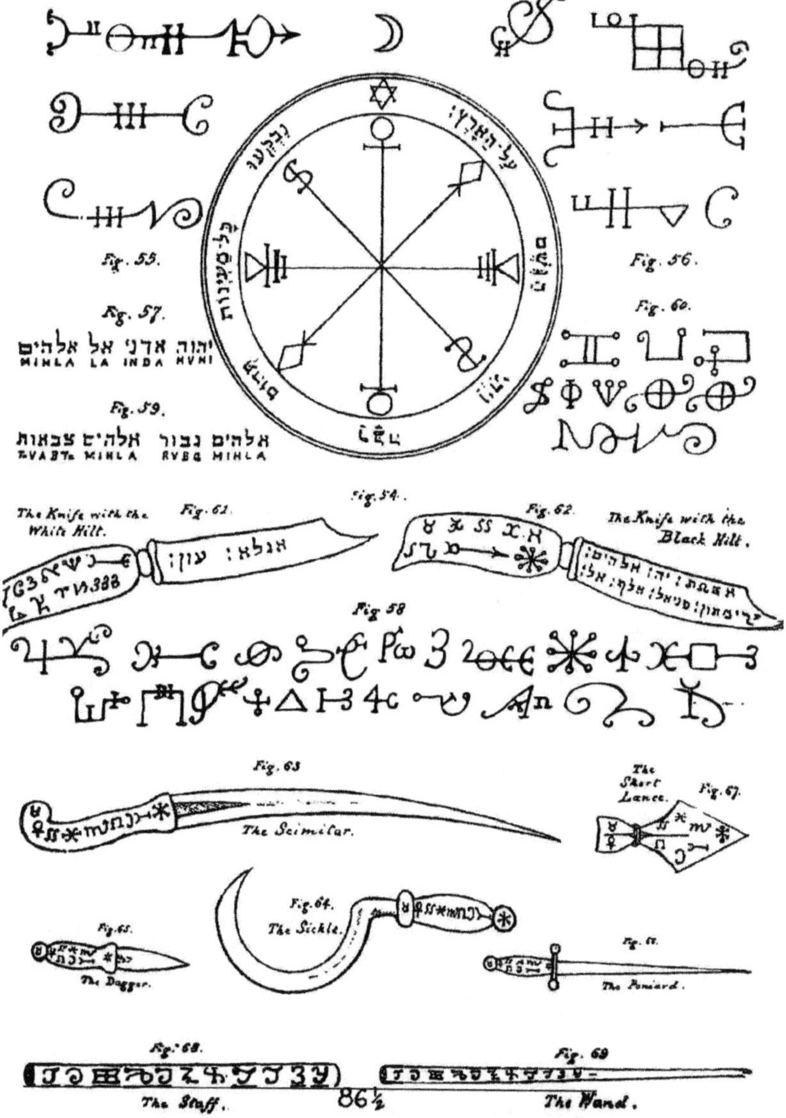

Fig. 55.
Fig. 56.
Fig. 57.
יהוה אדני אל אלהים
MIHLA LA INDA HVHI
Fig. 59.
אלהים גבור אלהים צבאות
RVBG MIHLA
Fig. 60.
Fig. 54.
The Knife with the White Hilt.
Fig. 61.
Fig. 62.
The Knife with the Black Hilt.
Fig. 58
Fig. 63
The Scimitar.
The Short Lance.
Fig. 67.
Fig. 64.
The Sickle.
Fig. 65.
The Dagger.
The Poniard.
Fig. 68.
The Staff.
Fig. 69
The Wand.

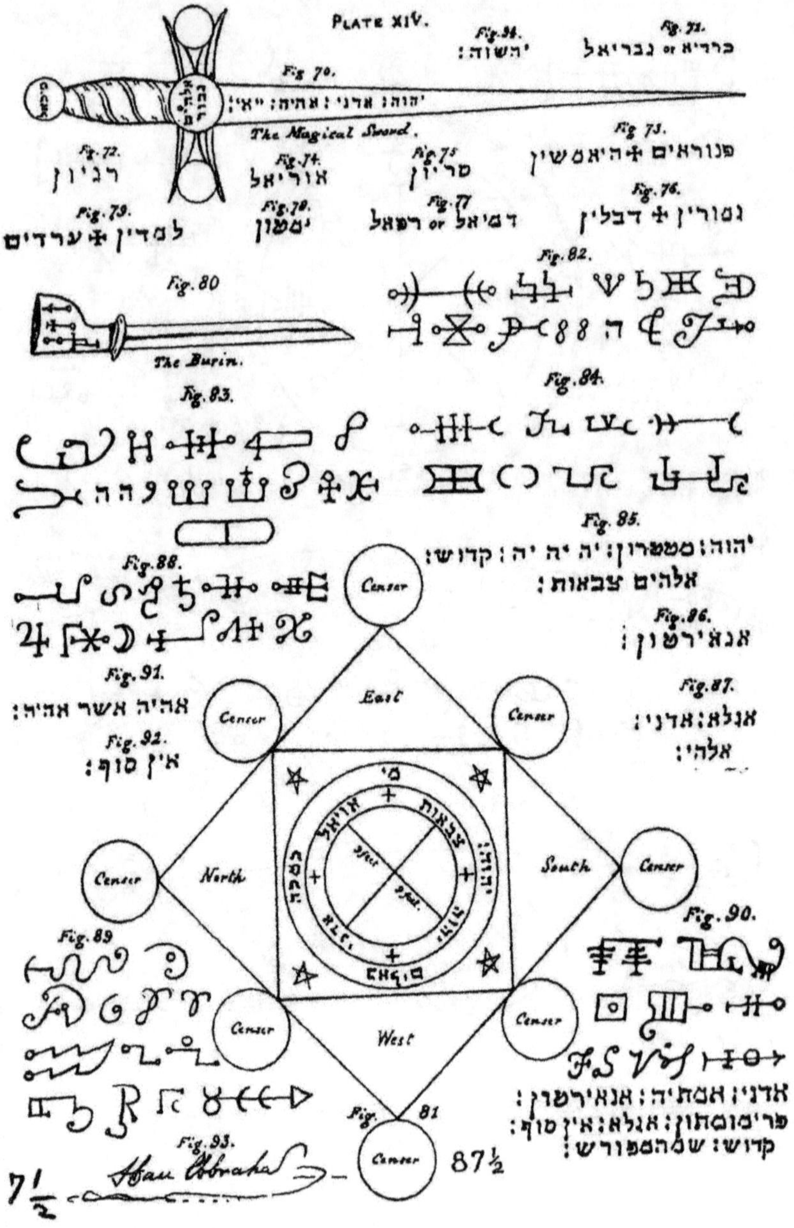
PLATE XIV.
Fig. 70.
The Magical Sword.
Fig. 71.
Fig. 72.
Fig. 73.
Fig. 74.
אוריאל
Fig. 75
סריון
Fig. 76.
Fig. 77
Fig. 78.
Fig. 79.
Fig. 80
The Burin.
Fig. 82.
Fig. 83.
Fig. 84.
Fig. 85.
אלהים צבאות:
Fig. 86.
Fig. 87.
אגלא: אדני:
אלהי:
Fig. 88.
Fig. 89
Fig. 90.
Fig. 91.
אהיה אשר אהיה:
Fig. 92.
אין סוף:
Fig. 93.
Fig. 94.
Censer
East
North
South
West
Fig. 81
87½
7½

be traced thereon. Thou shalt perfume them according to the rules of Art; and wrap them in silk cloth like the others.

The Staff (*see Figure* 68) should be of elderwood, or cane, or rosewood; and the Wand (*Figure* 69) of hazel or nut tree, in all cases the wood being virgin, that is of one year's growth only. They should each be cut from the tree at a single stroke, on the day of Mercury, at sunrise. The characters shown should be written or engraved thereon in the day and hour of Mercury.

This being done, thou shalt say:—

ADONAI, Most Holy, deign to bless and to consecrate this Wand, and this Staff, that they may obtain the necessary virtue, through Thee, O Most Holy ADONAI, whose kingdom endureth unto the Ages of the Ages. Amen.

After having perfumed and consecrated them, put them aside in a pure and clean place for use when required.

Swords are also frequently necessary for use in Magical Arts. Thou shalt therefore take a new Sword which thou shalt clean and polish on th day of Mercury, and at the first or the fifteenth hour, and after this thou shalt write on one side these Divine Names in Hebrew, YOD HE VAU HE, ADONAI, EHEIEH, YAYAI; and on the other side ELOHIM GIBOR (*see Figure* 70); sprinkle and cense it and repeat over it the following conjuration:—

THE CONJURATION OF THE SWORD.

I conjure thee, O Sword, by these Names, ABRAHACH, ABRACH, ABRACADABRA, YOD HE VAU HE, that thou serve me for a strength and defence in all Magical Operations, against all mine Enemies, visible and invisible.

I conjure thee anew by the Holy and Indivisible Name of EL strong and wonderful; by the Name SHADDAI Almighty; and by these Names QADOSCH, QADOSCH, QADOSCH, ADONAI ELOHIM TZABAOTH, EMANUEL, the First and the Last, Wisdom, Way, Life, Truth, Chief, Speech, Word, Splendour, Light, Sun, Fountain, Glory, the Stone of the Wise, Virtue, Shepherd, Priest, Messiach Immortal; by these Names then, and by the other Names, I conjure thee, O Sword, that thou servest me for a Protection in all adversities. Amen.

This being finished thou shalt wrap it also in silk like all the other Instruments, being duly purified and consecrated by the Ceremonies requisite for the perfection of all Magical Arts and Operations.

Three* other Swords should be made for the use of the Disciples.

The first one should have on the pommel the Name CARDIEL or GABRIEL (*see Figure* 71); on the Lamen of the Guard, REGION (*Figure* 72); on the Blade, PANORAIM HEAMESIN (*Figure* 73).

The Second should have on the pommel the Name AURIEL (*Figure*

* The description of these three Swords for the Disciples is only given in 1307 Sloane MSS.

74); on the Lamen of the Guard, SARION (*Figure* 75); on the Blade. GAMORIN DEBALIN (*Figure* 76).

The third should have on the pommel the Name DAMIEL or RAPHAEL (*Figure* 77); on the Lamen of the Guard, YEMETON (*Figure* 78); on the Blade, LAMEDIN ERADIM (*Figure* 79).

The Burin* (*Figure* 80) or Graver is useful for engraving or incising characters. In the day and hour either of Mars or of Venus thou shalt engrave thereon the characters shown, and having sprinkled and censed it thou shalt repeat over it the following Prayer:—

PRAYER.

ASOPHIEL, ASOPHIEL, ASOPHIEL, PENTAGRAMMATON, ATHANATOS, EHEIEH ASHER EHEIEH, QADOSCH, QADOSCH, QADOSCH; O God Eternal, and my Father, bless this Instrument prepared in Thine honour, so that it may only serve for a good use and end, for Thy Glory. Amen.

Having again perfumed, thou shalt put it aside for use. The Needle may be consecrated in the same way.

* From here to the end of the Chapter is from 1203 Lansdowne MSS.

BOOK TWO.

CHAPTER IX.

Of the Formation of the Circle.

Having chosen a place for preparing and constructing the Circle,* and all things necessary being prepared for the perfection of the Operations, take thou the Sickle or Scimitar of Art and stick it into the centre of the place where the Circle is to be made; then take a cord of nine feet in length, fasten one end thereof unto the Sickle and with the other end trace out the circumference of the Circle, which may be marked either with the Sword or with the Knife with the Black hilt. Then within the Circle mark out four regions, namely, towards the East, West, South, and North, wherein place Symbols; and beyond the limits of this Circle describe with the Consecrated Knife or Sword another Circle, but leaving an open space therein towards the North whereby thou mayest enter and depart beyond the Circle of Art. Beyond this again thou shalt describe another Circle at a foot distance with the aforesaid Instrument, yet ever leaving therein an open space for entrance and egress corresponding to the open space already left in the other. Beyond this again make another Circle at another foot distance, and beyond these two Circles, which are beyond the Circle of Art yet upon the same Centre, thou shalt describe Pentagrams with the Symbols and Names of the Creator therein so that they may surround the Circle already described. Without these Circles shalt thou circumscribe a Square, and beyond that another Square, so that the Angles of the former may touch the centres of the sides of the latter, and that the Angles of the latter may stretch towards the four quarters of the Universe, East, West, North, and South; and at the four Angles of each square, and touching them, thou shalt describe lesser Circles wherein let there be placed standing censers with lighted charcoal and sweet odours.

These things being done, let the Magus of Art† assemble his Disciples, exhort, confirm, and cheer them; lead them into the Circle of Art and station them therein towards the Four Quarters of the Universe, exhort them to fear nothing, and to abide in their assigned places. Furthermore let each of the Companions have a Sword besides the Sword of the Art, which he must hold naked in his hand. Then let the Magus quit the Circle, and Kindle the Censers, and place thereon exorcised Incense, as is said in the Chapter of Fumigations; and let him have the Censers in his

* This Chapter is only given in 10,862 Add. MSS.
† "Maghus" in MS. not "Magister."

hand and kindle it, and then place it in the part prepared. Let him now enter within the Circle and carefully close the openings left in the same, and let him again warn his Disciples, and take the Trumpet of Art prepared as is said in the Chapter concerning the same, and let him incense the Circle towards the Four Quarters of the Universe.

After this let the Magus commence his Incantations, having placed the Sickle, Sword, or other Implement of Art upright in the ground at his feet. Having sounded the trumpet as before taught let him invoke the Spirits, and if need be conjure them, as is said in the First Book, and having attained his desired effect, let him license them to depart.

Here followeth the Form of the Circle (*see Figure* 81), wherein whosoever entereth he shall be at safety as within a fortified Castle, and nothing shall be able to harm him.

BOOK TWO.

CHAPTER X.

Concerning Incense, Suffumigations, Perfumes, Odours, and Similar Things Which Are Used in Magical Arts.

There are many kinds of *Incense*, *Suffumigations*, and *Perfumes*, which are made for and offered unto the Spirits; those which are of sweet odour are for the good, those which are of evil savour are for the evil.

For perfumes of good odour, take thou aloes, nutmeg, gum benjamin, musk, and make a mixture which will give off a good perfume.

Editor's Note.—The advanced *Occult* student, and *Disciple of Magical Art*, use Vale of Kashmar, the great *Oriental Perfume*, today, instead of the spices mentioned herein. Vale of Kashmar Perfume, owing to its pure and beautiful fragrance, strength, and virtue, is believed to possess wonderful power to attract the *Good Spirits* and banish the *Evil Ones*, and for this very reason is now generally used in all invocations instead of the spices mentioned above. The *Disciple*, of course, can use which he or she chooses, but in case it be not easy or convenient to obtain the spices then you may send to Messrs. de Laurence, Scott & Co., for *Order No.* 504, for a bottle of Vale Of Kashmar, The *Great Oriental Perfume*. The very same gives forth a subtle, powerful, and beautifully fragrant *Oriental* odor.

For a suitable Suffumigation, thou may burn *Temple Incense*, as it gives forth a most fragrant odour which seems to possess the power to attract the *Good Spirits*, and force the *Evil Ones* to go away from thee; over which thou shalt say:—

THE EXORCISM OF TEMPLE INCENSE.

O God of Abraham, God of Isaac, God of Jacob, deign to bless this odoriferous Incense so that it may receive strength, virtue, and power to attract the *Good Spirits*, and to banish and cause to retire all hostile *Phantoms*. Through Thee, O Most *Holy Adonai*, Who livest and reignest unto the Ages of the Ages. Amen.

I exorcise thee, O Spirit impure and unclean, thou who art a hostile *Phantom*, in the Name of God, that thou quit this *Temple Incense*, thou and all thy deceits, that it may be consecrated and sanctified in the name of God Almighty. May the Holy Spirit of God grant protection and virtue unto those who use *Temple Incense;* and may the hostile and *Evil Spirit* and *Phantom* never be able to enter therein, through the Ineffable Name of God Almighty. *Amen.*

O Lord, deign to bless and to sanctify this *Sacred Incense* so that it may be a remedy unto mankind for the health of body and of soul, through the Invocation of Thy Holy Name. May all Creatures who receive the odour of this *Incense* and of these spices* receive health of body and of soul,through Him Who hath formed the Ages. *Amen.*

After this thou shalt sprinkle the various Spices (or the perfumed handkerchief spoken of in Foot Note below) with the Water of the Art, and thou shalt place them aside in a piece of silk as in other cases, or in a box destined for the purpose, so that thou mayest have them ready prepared for use when necessary.

When thou wishest to use the *Temple Incense,* thou shalt kindle a fire of fresh Incense, in an *Incense Burner,* and the Incense being lighted thou shalt say over it as follows, before putting the Spices or Perfumed handkerchief beside the *Incense Burner:*—

THE EXORCISM OF THE FIRE.

I exorcise thee, O Creature of Fire, by Him through Whom all things have been made, so that every kind of Phantasm may retire from thee, and be unable to harm or deceive in any way, through the Invocation of the Most High Creator of all. Amen.

Bless, O Lord All-Powerful, and All-Merciful, this Creature of Fire, so that being blessed by Thee, it may be for the honour and glory of Thy Most Holy Name, so that it may work no hindrance or evil unto those who use it. Through Thee, O Eternal and Almighty Lord, and through Thy Most Holy Name. Amen.

This being done, thou shalt put the Spices upon the Fire, and make what perfumes and suffumigations thou requirest.

Over Fumigations of evil odour thou shalt say:—

ADONAI, LAZAI, DALMAI, AIMA, ELOHI, O Holy Father, grant unto us succour, favour, and grace, by the Invocation of thy Holy Name, so that these things may serve us for aid in all that we wish to perform therewith, that all deceit may quit them, and that they may be blessed and sanctified through Thy Name. Amen.

* **Vale of Kashmar, The Great Oriental Perfume, may be used by sprinkling it on a clean handkerchief and placing it beside the Incense, instead of the spices if you prefer it.**

BOOK TWO.

CHAPTER XI.

Of the Water, and of the Hyssop.

If it be necessary to sprinkle with water anything required in the Art it should be done with a Sprinkler.

Prepare a Censer in the day and hour of Mercury, with the odoriferous Spices of the Art. After this thou shalt take a vessel of brass, of lead varnished within and without, or of earth, which thou shalt fill with most clear spring water, and thou shalt have salt, and say these words over the salt:—

Tzabaoth, Messiach, Emanuel, Elohim Gibor, Yod He Vau He; O God, Who art the Truth and the Life, deign to bless and sanctify this Creature of Salt, to serve unto us for help, protection, and assistance in this Art, experiment, and operation, and may it be a succor unto us.

After this cast the salt into the vessel wherein is the Water, and say the following Psalms: cii.; liv.; vi.; lxvii.

Thou shalt then make unto thyself a Sprinkler of vervain, fennel, lavender, sage, valerian, mint, garden-basil, rosemary, and hyssop, gathered in the day and hour of Mercury, the moon being in her increase. Bind together these herbs with a thread spun by a young maiden, and engrave upon the handle on the one side the characters shown in *Figure* 82, and on the other side those given in *Figure* 83.

After this thou mayest use the Water, using the Sprinkler whenever it is necessary; and know that wheresoever thou shalt sprinkle this Water, it will chase away all Phantoms, and they shall be unable to hinder or annoy any. With this same Water thou shalt make all the preparations of the Art.

BOOK TWO.

CHAPTER XII.

Of the Light, and of the Fire.

It hath been ever the custom among all nations to use fire and light in sacred things. For this reason the Master of the Art should also employ them in sacred rites, and besides those for reading the Conjurations by, and for the incense, in all operations Lights are necessary in the Circle.

For this reason he should make candles of virgin wax in the day and hour of Mercury; the wicks should have been made by a young girl; and the Candles should be made when the moon is in her increase, of the weight of half a pound each, and on them thou shalt engrave these characters with the Dagger, or the Burin of Art. (*See Figure* 84.)

After this thou shalt repeat over the Candles, Psalms cli.; ciii.; cvii., and shalt say:—*

O Lord God, Who governest all things by Thine Almighty Power, give unto me, a poor sinner, understanding and knowledge to do only that which is agreeable unto Thee; grant unto me to fear, adore, love, praise and give thanks unto Thee with true and sincere faith and perfect charity. Grant, O Lord, before I die, and descend into the realms beneath, and before the fiery flame shall devour me, that Thy Grace may not leave me, O Lord of my Soul. Amen.

After this thou shalt add:—

I exorcise thee, O Creature of wax, by Him Who alone hath created all things by His Word, and by the virtue of Him Who is pure truth, that thou cast out from thee every Phantasm, Perversion, and Deceit of the Enemy, and may the Virtue and Power of God enter into thee, so that thou mayest give us light, and chase far from us all fear or terror.

After this thou shalt sprinkle them with the Water of the Art, and incense them with the usual perfumes.

And when thou shalt wish to kindle them thou shalt say:—

I exorcise thee, O Creature of Fire, in the Name of the Sovereign and Eternal Lord, by His Ineffable Name, which is Yod, He, Vau, He; by the Name Iah; and by the Name of Power El; that thou mayest enlighten the heart of all the Spirits which we shall call unto this Circle, so that they may appear before us without fraud and deceit through Him Who hath created all things.

Then thou shalt take a square Lantern, with panes of Crystal glass, and thou shalt fit therein the Candle lighted, to read by, to form the Circle, or any other purpose for which thou shalt require it.

* Special Waxen Candles may be obtained from Messrs. de Laurence, Scott & Co., if it is not convenient to construct the kind mentioned above. Many students are using the candles with good results. See Order No. 131.

BOOK TWO.

CHAPTER XIII.

Concerning the Precepts of the Art.

He who hath attained the rank or degree of Exorcist, which we are usually accustomed to call Magus or Master* according to grade, whensoever he desireth to undertake any operation, for the nine days immediately preceding the commencement of the work, should put aside from him all uncleanness, and prepare himself in secret during these days, and prepare all the things necessary, and in the space of these days all these should be made, consecrated, and exorcised.

The which being duly completed, let him go on the day and hour of the commencement of the work, unto the place set apart for the same, as hath been said, in the place concerning the formation of the Circle. Let him instruct his Disciples on no cause whatsoever to move from their assigned places. And the Magus should exhort them with a bold and confident voice as follows:—

THE EXHORTATION OF THE COMPANIONS.

Fear ye not, my beloved Companions, seeing that we draw near unto the desired end; therefore, all things being rightly done and the Conjurations and Exorcisms diligently performed, ye shall behold Kings of Kings, and Emperors of Emperors, and other Kings, Princes, and Majesties with them, and a great crowd of followers, together with all sorts of musical instruments, yet nothing should either the Magus or his Disciples fear.

And then let the Magus say:—

I exhort you by these Holy Names of God, Elohim, Adonai, Agla, that none of you now presume to move or cross over from your appointed stations.

This being said, let the *Magus* and his *Disciples* uncover the *Holy Pentacles* and show them towards each quarter, and they being shown in each place, there shall be noises and rushings.

Then shall the Emperor of (the Spirits) say unto you:—From the time of the Great Addus until now, there hath not been an Exorciser who could behold my person, and unless those things† which ye have showed unto us hath been made, ye would not now have seen me. But seeing that

* This Chapter is only given in 10,862 Add. MSS.
† The Pentacles.

ye have powerfully called us, as I believe, by the rites derived from Solomon, and which but few of your comrades, or Exorcisers, possess, also they compel us against our will, and I therefore say unto thee that we wish to be obedient in all matters.

Then shall the Magus place the petitions of himself and his companions, which should be written down clearly on virgin card, or paper, beyond the Çircle towards the King or Prince of the Spirits, and he will receive it and take counsel with his Chiefs. After this he will return the Card, saying:—That which thou desirest is accomplished, be thy will performed, and all thy demands fulfilled.

BOOK TWO.

CHAPTER XIV.

Of the Pen, Ink, and Colours.

All things employed for writing, &c., in this Art, should be prepared in the following manner:

Thou shalt take a male gosling, from which thou shalt pluck the third feather of the right wing, and in plucking it thou shalt say:—

Adrai, Hahlii, Tamaii, Tilonas, Athamas, Zianor, Adonai, banish from this pen all deceit and error, so that it may be of virtue and efficacy to write all that I desire. Amen.

After this thou shalt sharpen it with the penknife of the Art, perfume it, sprinkle it, and place it aside in a silken cloth.

Thou shalt have an Inkstand made of earth or any convenient matter, and in the day and hour of Mercury thou shalt engrave thereon with the Burin of Art these Names:—Yod, He, Vau, He, Metatron, Iah Iah Iah, Qadosch, Elohim Tzabaoth (*see Figure* 85); and in putting the ink therein thou shalt say:—

I exorcise thee, O Creature of Ink, by Anaireton, by Simulator, and by the Name Adonai, and by the Name of Him through Whom all things were made, that thou be unto me an aid and succor in all things which I wish to perform by thine aid.

As it sometimes happeneth that it is necessary to write with some noble color, it is well to have a new and clean box wherein to keep them. The principal colors will be Yellow or Gold, Red, Celestial or Azure Blue, Green, and Brown; and any other colors that may be requisite. Thou shalt exorcise, perfume, and sprinkle them in the usual manner.

BOOK TWO.

CHAPTER XV.

Of the Pen of the Swallow and of the Crow.

TAKE the feather of a Swallow or of a Crow, and before plucking it thou shalt say:—

May Holy MICHAEL the Archangel of God, and MIDAEL and MIRAEL, the Chiefs and Captains of the Celestial Army, be my aid in the operation I am about to perform, so that I may write herewith all things which are necessary, and that all the experiments which I commence herewith may through you and through your names be perfected by the power of the Most High Creator. Amen.

After this thou shalt point and complete the pen with the Knife of the Art, and with the pen and ink of the art thou shalt write upon its side the Name, ANAIRETON (*see Figure* 86), and thou shalt say over it the following Psalms: cxxxiii.; cxvii.

BOOK TWO.

CHAPTER XVI.

Of the Blood of the Bat, Pigeon, and Other Animals.

Take a living Bat and exorcise it thus:—

THE EXORCISM OF THE BAT.

CAMIACH, EOMIAHE, EMIAL, MACBAL, EMOII, ZAZEAN, MAIPHIAT, ZACRATH, TENDAC, VULAMAHI; by these Most Holy Names, and the other Names of Angels which are written in the Book ASSAMAIAN,* I conjure thee O Bat (or whatever animal it may be) that thou assist me in this operation, by God the True, God the Holy, the God Who hath created thee, and by Adam, Who hath imposed thy true name upon thee and upon all other animated beings.

After this, take the Needle or other convenient Instrument of Art, as will be said later on, and pierce the bat in the vein which is in the right wing; and collect the blood in a small vessel over the which thou shalt say:—

Almighty ADONAI, ARATHRON, ASHAI, ELOHIM, ELOHI, ELION, ASHER EHEIEH, SHADDAI, O God the Lord, immaculate, immutable, EMANUEL, MESSIACH, YOD, HE, VA'U, HE, be my aid, so that this blood may have power and efficacy in all wherein I shall wish, and in all that I shall demand.

Perfume it and keep it for use.

The blood of other winged animals may be taken in the same manner, with the proper solemnities.

I cannot too strongly impress on the readers of this volume that the use of blood is more or less connected with Black Magic; and that it should be avoided as much as possible.—DR. de LAURENCE.

* The "Sepher Ha-Shamaiim," or "Book of the Heavens."

BOOK TWO.

CHAPTER XVII.

OF VIRGIN PARCHMENT, OR VIRGIN PAPER, AND HOW IT SHOULD BE PREPARED.

VIRGIN *Parchment Paper,* made from the skin of dead-born lambs, which is new, pure, clean, and exorcised, never having served for any other purpose.

Genuine Virgin Parchment is necessary in many *Magical Operations,* and should be properly prepared and consecrated. There are two kinds, one called *Virgin,* the other *Unborn. Virgin Parchment* is that which is taken from an Animal which hath not attained the age of generation, whether it be ram, or kid, or other animal.

Unborn Parchment is taken from an animal which hath been taken before its time from the uterus of its mother.

Take whichsoever of these two classes of animals thou pleasest, provided only that it be male, and in the day and hour of Mercury; and take it to a secret place where no man may see thee at work. Thou shalt have a marsh-reed cut at a single stroke with a new knife, and thou shalt strip from it the leaves, repeating this Conjuration:—

THE CONJURATION OF THE REED.

I conjure thee by the Creator of all things, and by the King of Angels, Whose Name is EL SHADDAI, that thou receivest strength and virtue to flay this animal and to construct the parchment whereon I may write the Holy Names of God, and that it may acquire so great virtue that all which I shall write or do may obtain its effect, through Him who liveth unto the Eternal Ages. Amen.

Before cutting the Reed recite Psalm lxxii.:—

After this, with the Knife of the Art, thou shalt fashion the Reed into the shape of a Knife, and upon it thou shalt write these Names: AGLA, ADONAI, ELOHI (*see Figure* 87), through Whom be the work of this Knife accomplished. Then thou shalt say:—

O God, Who drewest Moses, Thy well-beloved and Thine elect, from among the Reeds on the marshy banks of the Nile, and from the Waters, he being yet but a child, grant unto me through Thy great mercy and compassion that this Reed may receive Power and Virtue to effect that which I desire through Thy Holy Name and the Names of Thy Holy Angels. Amen.

This being done, thou shalt commence with this Knife to flay the Animal, whether it be Virgin or Unborn, saying:—

ZOHAR, ZIO, TALMAÏ, ADONAI, SHADDAI, TETRAGRAMMATON, and

ye Holy Angels of God; be present, and grant power and virtue unto this parchment, and may it be consecrated by you, so that all things which I shall write thereon shall obtain their effect. Amen.

The Animal being flayed, take Salt, and say thus over it:—

God of Gods, and Lord of Lords, Who hast created all things from Negative Existence, deign to bless and sanctify this Salt, so that in placing it upon this parchment which I wish to make, it may have such virtue that whatsoever I may write on it hereafter may attain its desired end. Amen.

Afterwards rub the said parchment with the exorcised salt, and leave it in the Sun, to imbibe this salt for the space of an entire day. Then take a large earthen vessel glazed within and without, round the outside of which thou shalt write the characters in *Figure* 88.

After this thou shalt put powdered lime into the vessel, saying:—

OROII, ZARON, ZAINON, ZEVARON, ZAHIPHIL, ELION, be ye present and bless this work so that it may attain the desired effect, through the King of the Heavens, and the God of the Angels. Amen.

Take then exorcised Water and pour it upon the said lime, and place the skin therein for three days, after which thou shalt take it thence, and scrape therefrom the lime and flesh adhering, with the Knife of Reed.

After this thou shalt cut, with a single stroke, a Wand of Hazel, long enough for thee to form a Circle therewith; take also a cord spun by a young maiden, and small stones or pebbles from a brook, pronouncing these words:—

O God Adonai, Holy and Powerful Father, put virtue into these stones, that they may serve to stretch this parchment, and to chase therefrom all fraud, and may it obtain virtue by Thine Almighty Power.

After this, having stretched the said parchment upon the Circle and bound it with the cord and stones, thou shalt say:

AGLA, YOD, HE, VAU, HE, IAH, EMANUEL, bless and preserve this parchment, so that no Phantasm may enter therein.

Let it dry thus for three days in a dark and shady place, then cut the cord with the Knife of Art, and detach the Parchment from the Circle, saying.—

ANTOR, ANCOR, TURLOS, BEODONOS, PHAIAR, APHARCAR, be present for a guard unto this Parchment.

Then perfume it, and keep it in silk ready for use.

No woman, if her flowers be upon her, should be permitted to see this *Parchment*; otherwise it will lose its virtue. He who maketh it should be pure, clean, and prepared.

But if the preparation of the aforesaid parchment seemeth too tedious, thou mayest make it in the following manner, but it is not so good.

Take any Parchment, and exorcise it; prepare a censer with perfumes; write upon the parchment the characters in *Figure* 89, hold it over the Incense, and say:—

Be ye present to aid me, and may my operation be accomplished through you; ZAZAII, ZALMAII, DALMAII, ADONAI, ANAPHAXETON, CEDRION, CRIPON, PRION, ANAIRETON, ELION, OCTINOMON, ZEVANION, ALAZAION, ZIDEON, AGLA, ON, YOD HE VAU HE, ARTOR, DINOTOR, Holy Angels of God; be present and infuse virtue into this Parchment, so that it may obtain such power through you that all Names or Characters thereon written may receive due power, and that all deceit and hindrance may depart therefrom, through God the Lord merciful and gracious, Who liveth and reigneth through all the Ages. Amen.

Then shalt thou recite over the parchment Psalms lxxii.; cxvii.; and cxxiv.; and the *"Benedicite Omnia Opera."* Then say:—

I conjure thee, *O Virgin Parchment,* by all the Holy Names, that thou obtainest efficacy and strength, and becomest exorcised and consecrated, so that none of the things which may be written upon thee shall be effaced from the Book of Truth. Amen.

Then sprinkle it, and keep it as before said.

The Cauls of newly-born children, duly consecrated, may also be used instead of *Virgin Parchment.* Also paper, satin, silk, and the like substances, may be employed in operations of less importance if duly exorcised and consecrated.

BOOK TWO.

CHAPTER XVIII.

Of Wax and Virgin Earth.

Wax and Virgin Earth are also employed in many Magical Operations, whether to make Images, or Candles, or other things; therefore they should never have been put to any other use. The Earth should be dug up with thine own hands, and reduced to a paste, without touching it with any instrument whatever, so that it be not defiled thereby.

The Wax should be taken from bees which have only made it for the first time, and it should never have been employed for any other purpose; and when thou shalt wish it to avail thyself of the one or the other, thou shalt before commencing the work repeat the following conjuration:—

CONJURATION.

Extabor, Hetabor, Sittacibor, Adonai, Onzo, Zomen, Menor, Asmodal, Ascobai, Comatos, Erionas, Profas, Alkomas, Conamas, Papuendos, Osiandos, Espiacent, Damnath, Eheres, Golades, Telantes, Cophi, Zades, ye Angels of God be present, for I invoke ye in my work, so that through you it may find virtue and accomplishment. Amen.

After this repeat Psalms cxxxi.; xv.; cii.; viii.; lxxxiv.; lxviii.; lxxii.; cxxxiii.; cxiii.; cxxvi.; xlvi.; xlvii.; xxii.; li.; cxxx.; cxxxix.; xlix.; cx.; liii.; and say:—

I exorcise thee, O Creature of Wax (or of Earth), that through the Holy Name of God and His Holy Angels thou receive blessing, so that thou mayest be sanctified and blessed, and obtain the virtue which we desire, through the Most Holy Name of Adonai. Amen.

Sprinkle the wax and put it aside for use; but take note that the Earth which should be dug up with thy hands should be prepared every time thou hast need thereof.

BOOK TWO.

CHAPTER XIX.

Concerning the Needle and Other Iron Instruments.

There are several steel instruments necessary in various Operations, as a Needle to prick or to sew; a Burin, or instrument wherewith to engrave, &c.

Thou shalt make such instruments in the day and hour of Jupiter, and when it is finished thou shalt say: —

I conjure thee, O Instrument of Steel, by God the Father Almighty, by the Virtue of the Heavens, of the Stars, and of the Angels who preside over them; by the virtue of stones, herbs, and animals; by the virtue of hail, snow, and wind; that thou receivest such virtue that thou mayest obtain without deceit the end which I desire in all things where I shall use thee; through God the Creator of the Ages, and Emperor of the Angels. Amen.

Afterwards repeat Psalms iii.; ix.; xxxi.; xlii.; lx.; li.; cxxx.

Perfume it with the perfumes of the Art, and sprinkle it with exo cised water, wrap it in silk and say:—

Dani, Zumech, Agalmaturod, Gadiel, Pani, Caneloas, Merod, Gamidoi, Baldoi, Metrator, Angels most holy, be present for a guard unto this instrument.

BOOK TWO.

CHAPTER XX.

Concerning the Silken Cloth.

When any Instrument of the Art is properly consecrated, it should be wrapped in silk and put away, as we have said.

Take, then, silk of any color except black or grey, whereon write the words and Characters in *Figure* 90.

Perfume it with incense of good odor, sprinkle it, and recite Psalms lxxxii.; lxxii.; cxxxiv.; lxiv.

After this thou shalt put it aside for seven days with sweet spices; and thou shalt use this silk to wrap all the instruments of the Art.

BOOK TWO.

CHAPTER XXI.

Concerning Characters, and the Consecration of the Magical Book

Whensoever in any Operation it is necessary to write Characters, and thou fearest that thou wilt fail, do this: Write at the beginning the Name Eheieh Asher Eheieh (*Figure* 91), and at the end the name Ain Soph (*Figure* 92); between these Names write what thou wishest, and if thou hast anything especial to do bear the said written Names upon the wrapper in silk, and thou shalt say over them:—

Most Wise and Most High Creator of all things, I pray Thee for Thy grace and mercy that Thou mayest grant such virtue and power unto these Holy Names, that Thou mayest keep these characters from all deceit and error, through Thee, O Most Holy Adonai. Amen.

After having repeated this thou shalt write the requisite Characters, and thou shalt not fail, but shall attain thy desired end.

THE CONSECRATION OF THE BOOK.

Make a Book, containing sixteen pages, from Virgin Parchment, and write therein, with red ink, the Prayers for all the Operations,* the Names of the Angels in the form of Litanies, their Seals and Characters; the which being done thou shalt consecrate the same unto God and unto the pure Spirits in the manner following:—

Thou shalt set in the destined place a small table covered with a white cloth, whereon thou shalt lay the Book opened at the *Great Pentacle* which should be drawn on the first leaf of the said Book; and having kindled a lamp which should be suspended above the center of the table, thou shalt surround the said table with a white curtain; clothe thyself in the proper vestments, and holding the Book open, repeat upon thy knees the following prayer with great humility:—

(For the Prayer beginning "Adonai Elohim," &c., see Book I., Chapter XIV., where it is given in full.)

After which thou shalt incense it with the incense proper to the Planet and the day, and thou shalt replace the Book on the aforesaid Table, taking heed that the fire of the lamp be kept up continually during the operation, and keeping the curtains closed. Repeat the same ceremony for seven days, beginning with Saturday, and perfuming the Book each day with the Incense proper to the Planet ruling the day and hour, and taking heed that the lamp shall burn both day and night; after the

* The rest of this Chapter is from 1203 Lansdowne MSS.

which thou shalt shut up the Book in a small drawer under the table, made expressly for it, until thou shalt have occasion to use it; and every time that thou wishest to use it, clothe thyself with thy vestments, kindle the lamp, and repeat upon thy knees the aforesaid prayer, *"Adonai Elohim."* &c.

It is necessary also, in the Consecration of the Book, to summon all the Angels whose Names are written therein in the form of Litanies, the which thou shalt do with devotion; and even if the Angels and Spirits appear not in the Consecration of the Book, be not thou astonished thereat, seeing that they are of a pure nature, and consequently have much difficulty in familiarizing themselves with men who are inconstant and impure, but the Ceremonies and Characters being correctly carried out devoutedly and with perseverance, they will be constrained to come, and it will at length happen that at thy first invocation thou wilt be able to see and communicate with them. But I advise thee to undertake nothing unclean or impure, for then thy importunity, far from attracting them, will only serve to chase them from thee; and it will be thereafter exceedingly difficult for thee to attract them for use for pure ends.

BOOK TWO.

CHAPTER XXII.

Concerning Sacrifices to the Spirits, and How They Should Be Made.

In many operations it is necessary to make some sort of sacrifice unto the Demons, and in various ways. Sometimes white animals are sacrificed to the good Spirits and black to the evil. Such sacrifices consist of the blood and sometimes of the flesh.

They who sacrifice animals, of whatsoever kind they be, should select those which are virgin, as being more agreeable unto the Spirits, and rendering them more obedient.

When blood is to be sacrificed it should be drawn also from virgin quadrupeds or birds, but before offering the oblation, say:—

May this Sacrifice which we find it proper to offer unto ye, noble and lofty Beings, be agreeable and pleasing unto your desires; be ye ready to obey us, and ye shall receive greater ones.

Then perfume and sprinkle it according to the rules of Art.

When it is necessary, with all the proper Ceremonies, to make Sacrifices of fire, they should be made of wood which hath some quality referring especially unto the Spirits invoked; as juniper of pine unto the Spirits of Saturn; box, or oak, unto those of Jupiter; cornel, or cedar, unto those of Mars; laurel unto those of the Sun; myrtle unto those of Venus; hazel unto those of Mercury; and willow unto those of the Moon.

But when we make sacrifices of food and drink, everything necessary should be prepared without the circle, and the meats should be covered with some fine clean cloth, and have also a clean white cloth spread beneath them; with new bread and good and sparkling wine, but in all things those which refer to the nature of the Planet. Animals, such as fowls or pigeons, should be roasted. Especially shouldst thou have a vessel of clear and pure fountain water, and before thou enterest into the Circle, thou shalt summon the Spirits by their proper Names, or at least those chief among them, saying:—

In whatsoever place ye may be, ye Spirits, who are invited to this feast, come ye and be ready to receive our offerings, presents, and sacrifices, and ye shall have hereafter yet more agreeable oblations.

First perfume the room by burning Temple Incense therein, and sprinkle the viands with *exorcised water;* then commence to conjure the Spirits until they shall come.

This is the manner of making sacrifices in all arts and operations wherein it is necessary, and acting thus, the Spirits will be prompt to serve thee.

Here endeth our "*Key,*" the which if thou thoroughly instillest into thy memory, thou shalt be able, if it pleaseth thee, even to fly with the wings of the wind. But if thou takest little heed hereof, and despiseth this Book, never shalt thou attain unto the desired end in any Magical experiment or operation whatsoever.

For in this Book is comprised all science of Magical Art, and it should be strictly kept by thee. And hereunto is the end of our "*Key,*" in the Name of God the righteous, the merciful, and the eternal, Who liveth and reigneth throughout the Ages. Amen.

THE END OF THE KEY OF SOLOMON THE KING.

ANCIENT FRAGMENT OF THE KEY OF SOLOMON,

TRANSLATED FROM THE HEBREW BY ELIPHAZ LEVI; *And Given In His "Philosophe Occulte."—Serie II, Page 136.*

I will now give unto thee the Key of the Kingdom of the Spirits.

This Key is the same as that of the Mysterious Numbers of Yetzirah.*

The Spirits are governed by the natural and universal Hierarchy of things.

Three command Three through the medium of Three.

There are the Spirits of Above, those of Below, and those of the Center; then if thou investest the Sacred Ladder, if thou descendest instead of ascending, thou wilt discover the Counter-Hierarchy of the Shells, or of the Dead Spirits.

Know thou only that the Principalities of Heaven, the Virtues, and the Powers, are not Persons, but dignities.

They are the Degrees of the Sacred Ladder upon which the Spirits ascend and descend.

Michael, Gabriel, Raphael, and the others, are not Names but Titles.

The First of the Numbers is the Unity.

The First of the Divine Conceptions called the *Sephiroth* is Kether or the Crown.

The First Category of the Spirits is that of Chaioth Ha-Qadesh or the Intelligences of the Divine Tetragram, whose Letters are symbolized by the Mysterious Animals in the Prophecy of Ezekiel.

Their empire is that of unity and synthesis. They correspond to the Intelligence.

They have for adversaries the *Thamiel* or Double-Headed Ones, the Demons of revolt and of anarchy, whose two Chiefs, ever at War with each other, are *Satan* and *Moloch.*

The Second Number is two; the Second Sephira is Chokmah or Wisdom.

The Spirits of Wisdom are the Auphanim, a Name which signifieth the Wheels, because all acts in Heaven like immense Wheels spangled with Stars. Their Empire is that of Harmony. They correspond to the Reason.

* The "Sepher Yetzirah," or "Book of Formation," one of the most ancient Books of the Qabalah.

They have for Adversaries the *Chaigidel*, or the Shells which attach themselves to Material and Lying Appearances. Their Chief, or rather their Guide, for Evil Spirits obey no one, is *Beelzebub,* whose Name signifieth the God of Flies, because Flies haunt putrefying corpses.

The third Number is three. The third Sephira is Binah or Understanding.

The Spirits of Binah are Aralim, or the Strong. Their empire is the creation of ideas; they correspond to activity and energy of thought.

They have for adversaries the *Satariel,* or concealers, the Demons of absurdity, of intellectual inertia, and of Mystery. The Chief of the *Satariel* is *Lucifuge,* called falsely and by anti-phrase *Lucifer* (as the Eumenides, who are the Furies, are called in Greek the Gracious Ones).

The fourth Number is four. The fourth Sephira is Gedulah or Chesed, Magnificence or Mercy.

The Spirits of Gedulah are the Chaschmalim, or the Lucid Ones. Their empire is that of beneficence; they correspond to the imagination.

They have for adversaries the *Gamchicoth* or the Disturbers of Souls. The Chief or Guide of these Demons is *Ashtaroth* or *Astarte,* the impure Venus of the Syrians, whom they represent with the head of an ass or of a bull, and the breasts of a woman.

The fifth Number is five. The fifth Sephira is Geburah or Justice.

The Spirits of Geburah are the Seraphim, or the Spirits burning with zeal. Their empire is that of the chastisement of crimes. They correspond to the faculty of comparing and of choosing.

They have for adversaries the *Golab or incendiaries,* Genii of wrath and sedition, whose Chief is *Asmodeus,* whom they also call Samael the Black.

The sixth Number is six. The sixth Sephira is Tiphereth the Supreme Beauty.

The Spirits of Tiphereth are the Malachim, or the Kings. Their empire is that of the Universal Harmony. They correspond to the judgment.

They have for adversaries the *Tagaririm,* or Disputers, whose Chief is *Belphegor.*

The seventh Number is seven. The seventh Sephira is Netzach, or Victory.

The Spirits of Netzach is the Elohim or the Gods, that is to say the representatives of God. Their empire is that of progress and of life; they correspond to the *Sensorium* or to sensibility.

They have for adversaries the *Harab-Serapel,* or the Ravens of Death, whose Chief is Baal.

The eighth Number is eight. The eighth Sephira is Hod or eternal order.

The Spirits of Hod are the Beni-Elohim or Sons of the Gods. Their empire is that of order; they correspond to the inner sense.

They have for adversaries the *Samael* or jugglers, whose Chief is *Adramelech.*

The ninth Number is nine. The ninth Sephira is Yesod, or the fundamental principle.

The Spirits of Yesod are the Cherubim or Angels, those powers which fecundate the earth, and which are represented in Hebrew symbolism under the form of bulls. Their empire is that of fecundity. They correspond to true ideas.

They have for adversaries the *Gamaliel* or obscene, whose Queen is *Lilith,* the Demon of debaucheries.

The tenth Number is ten. The tenth Sephira is Malkuth, or the kingdom of forms.

The Spirits of Malkuth are the Ischim, or the virile ones; they are the souls of the Saints whose Chief is Moses. (Let us not forget that it is Solomon who speaks.—Eliphaz Lévi.)

They have for adversaries the wicked ones who obey *Nahema,* the Demon of Impurity.

The wicked are symbolized by the five accursed nations whom Joshua was to destroy.

Joshua, or Jehoshua the Saviour, is a symbol of the Messiach.

His Name is composed of the letters of the Divine Tetragram changed into the Pentagram by the addition of the Letter Schin (*see Figure* 94).

Each letter of this Pentagram represents a power of good attacked by the five accursed nations.

For the real history of the people of God is the allegorical legend of Humanity.

The five accursed nations are:—

1. The Amalekites or Aggressors;
2. The Geburim or Violent Ones;
3. The Raphaim or Cowards;
4. The Nephilim or Voluptuous Ones;
5. The Anakim or Anarchists.

The Anarchists are vanquished by the Yod, which is the Sceptre of the Father.

The Violent are vanquished by the Hé, which is the Gentleness of the Mother.

The Cowards are vanquished by the Vau, which is the Sword of Michael, and Generation by travail and pain.

The Voluptuous are vanquished by the second Hé, which is the painful bringing forth of the Mother.

Lastly, the Aggressors are vanquished by the Schin, which is the Fire of the Lord and the equilibrating Law of Justice.

The Princes of the Perverse Spirits are the False Gods whom they adore.

Hell has then no other government than that fatal law which punishes perversity and corrects error, for the false Gods only exist in the false opinion of their adorers.

Baal, Belphegor, Moloch, Adramelech, have been the idols of the Syrians; idols without soul, idols now destroyed, and of whom the Name alone remaineth.

The True God hath vanquished all the Demons as Truth triumphs over Error. That is past in the opinions of men, and the Wars of Michael against Satan are the symbols of movement, and of the progress of Spirits.

The Devil is ever a God of refusal.

Accredited idolatries are religions in their time.

Superannuated idolatries are Superstitions and Sacrileges.

The Pantheon of Phantoms, which are then in vogue, is the Heaven of the Ignorant.

The Receptacle of Phantoms, whom Folly even wisheth for no longer, is the Hell.

But all this existeth only in the Imagination of the Vulgar.

For the Wise, Heaven is the Supreme Reason, and Hell is Folly.

But it must be understood that we here employ the word Heaven in the Mystical sense which we give it in opposing to it the word Hell.

In order to evoke Phantoms it is sufficient to intoxicate oneself or to render oneself mad; for Phantoms are ever the companions of drunken-ness and of vertigo.

The Phosphorus of the imagination, abandoned to all the caprices of over-excited and diseased nerves, fills itself with Monsters and absurd visions.

We can also arrive at hallucination by mingling together wakeful-ness and sleep by the graduated use of narcotics; but such actions are crimes against nature.

Wisdom chaseth away Phantoms, and enables us to communicate with the Superior Spirits by the contemplation of the Laws of Nature and the study of the Holy Numbers.

(Here King Solomon addresseth himself to his son, Roboam) :-Do thou, O my son Roboam, remember, that the Fear of Adonai is only the beginning of Wisdom.

Keep and preserve those who have not Understanding in the Fear of Adonai, which will give and will preserve unto thee my crown.

But learn to triumph thyself over Fear by Wisdom, and the Spirits will descend from Heaven to serve thee.

I, SOLOMON, thy father, King of Israel and of Palmyra, I have sought out and obtained in my lot the Holy Chokmah, which is the Wis-dom of Adonai.

And I have become King of the Spirits as well of Heaven as of Earth, Master of the Dwellers of the Air, and of the Living Souls of the Sea, because I was in possession of the Key of the Hidden Gates of Light.

I have done great things by the virtue of the Schema Hamphorasch, and by the Thirty-two Paths of Yetzirah.

Number, weight, and measure determine the form of things; the substance is one, and God createth it eternally.

Happy is he who comprehendeth the Letters and the Numbers.

The Letters are from the Numbers, and the Numbers from the Ideas, and the Ideas from the Forces, and the Forces from the Elohim. The Synthesis of the Elohim is the Schema.

The Schema is one, its columns are two, its power is three, its form is four, its reflection giveth eight, which multiplied by three giveth unto thee the twenty-four Thrones of Wisdom.

Upon each Throne reposeth a Crown with three Rays, each Ray beareth a Name, each Name is an Absolute Idea. There are Seventy-two Names upon the Twenty-four Crowns of the Schema.

Thou shalt write these Names upon Thirty-six Talismans, two upon each Talisman, one on each side.

Thou shalt divide these Talismans into four series of nine each, according to the number of the Letters of the Schema.

Upon the first Series thou shalt engrave the Letter Yod, symbolized by the Flowering Rod of Aaron.

Upon the second the Letter Hé, symbolized by the Cup of Joseph.

Upon the third the Letter Vau, symbolized by the Sword of David my father.

And upon the fourth the Hé final, symbolized by the Shekel of Gold.

These thirty-six Talismans will be a Book which will contain all the Secrets of Nature. And by their diverse combinations thou shalt make the Genii and Angels speak.

HERE ENDETH THE FRAGMENT OF THE KEY OF SOLOMON.

PLATE XV.

The Mystical Alphabets.

114½

Hebrew Alphabet.
Alphabet of the Magi.
The Characters of Celestial Writing.
Malachim or the Writing of the Angels
The Writing called "Passing the River."
Names of the Letters.
The Powers of the Letters.
Finals.
Another form of Samekh
Aleph Samekh a' s
Beth Ayin b bh v o aa ng
Gimel Pé g gh p ph
Daleth Tzaddi d dh th tz
He' Qoph h' q qh
Vau Resh v u o r
Zaïn Schin z s sh
Cheth Tau ch gutt. t th
Teth t
Yod Final Kaph i y k
Kaph Final Mem k kh m
Lamed Final Nun l n
Mem Final Pé m p
Nun Final Tzaddi n tz

THE QABALISTICAL INVOCATION OF SOLOMON.

Given by Eliphaz Lévi in "Rituel de la Haute Magie," Chapter xiii.

POWERS of the Kingdom, be beneath my left foot, and within my right hand.

Glory and Eternity touch my shoulders, and guide me in the Paths of Victory.

Mercy and Justice be ye the Equilibrium and splendor of my life.

Understanding and Wisdom give unto me the Crown.

Spirits of Malkuth conduct me between the two columns whereon is supported the whole edifice of the Temple.

Angels of Netzach and of Hod strengthen me upon the Cubical Stone of Yesod.

O GEDULAHEL! O GEBURAHEL! O TIPHERETH!

BINAHEL, be Thou my Love!

RUACH CHOKMAHEL, be Thou my Light!

Be that which Thou art, and that which Thou willest to be, O KETHERIEL!

Ishim, assist me in the Name of SHADDAI.

Cherubim, be my strength in the Name of ADONAI.

Beni Elohim, be ye my brethren in the Name of the Son, and by the virtues of TZABAOTH.

Elohim, fight for me in the Name of TETRAGRAMMATON.

Malachim, protect me in the Name of YOD HE VAU HE.

Seraphim, purify my love in the Name of ELOAH.

Chaschmalim, enlighten me with the splendors of ELOHI, and of SCHECHINAH.

Aralim, act ye; *Auphanim*, revolve and shine.

Chaioth Ha-Qadosch, cry aloud, speak, roar, and groan; Qadosch, Qadosch, Qadosch, SHADDAI, ADONAI, YOD CHAVAH, EHEIEH ASHER EHEIEH!

Halelu-Yah! Halelu-Yah! Halelu-Yah. Amen.

www.ingramcontent.com/pod-product-compliance
Lightning Source LLC
LaVergne TN
LVHW051641080426
835511LV00016B/2432
* 9 7 8 1 6 3 9 2 3 1 8 6 7 *